RETHINK LOVE

Rethink series:

Rethink

love

3 STEPS TO BEING THE ONE,

ATTRACTING THE ONE, AND BECOMING ONE

MONICA BERG

No part of this publication may be reproduced or transmitted in any form or
by any means, electronic or mechanical, including photocopying, recording,
or by any information storage and retrieval system, without permission in
writing from the publisher, except by a reviewer who wishes to quote brief
passages in connection with a review written for inclusion in a magazine,
newspaper, or broadcast.

Kabbalah Centre Publishing is a registered DBA of
Kabbalah Centre International, Inc.

For further information:

The Kabbalah Centre
1062 S. Robertson Blvd., Los Angeles, CA 90035
155 E. 48th St., New York, NY 10017

1.800.Kabbalah www.kabbalah.com

Printed in USA , Feb 2020

ISBN: 978-1-57189-998-9

I lovingly dedicate this book to my husband, Michael.

"Here is the deepest secret nobody knows

(here is the root of the root and the bud

of the bud and the sky of the sky of a tree

called life; which grows higher than soul

can hope or mind can hide) and this is the

wonder that's keeping the stars apart"

I carry your heart (I carry it in my heart)

— E.E. Cummings

Dearest, darling, forever, always...

Michael, I can wholeheartedly say that we have grown so much together. The people we have become are so different, better and more in love than the people who were married 22 years ago.

Everything with you is better. You are home to me.

It's not the big things you do, but rather the little things that move my heart so profoundly.

When I married you, I felt like I was starting a new life, with endless possibilities, opportunities, excitement, and work (the good kind), which consists of finding purpose and pursuing freedom.

I found an old anniversary card that you wrote to me:
"Of course, you are not perfect, nobody is meant to be. But it is often in your failings and faults that the best parts of you are revealed. I hope one day you can see you as I do, and to appreciate who you are as much as I do."

Michael, you give me the strength, support, and vision to dare, to want more, to do more, and to be more.

Love you more,
Monica

With gratitude

Thank you Alex, from the bottom of my heart, for making the printing of this book possible. The world needs more angels like you.

— Monica

"May the light and wisdom from this book help many practice and live lives of true love in order to quickly bring a world of peace."

With gratitude,

Alex Nimick

Table of Contents

Conclusion: The ~~End~~ Beginning

Introduction

There's only one way to receive love, and that's to give it away.

I've attended more than 500 weddings over 20 years, and I've been privy to couples' most intimate moments, as they share their hopes and fears about marriage before the ceremony, and as they work through the inevitable issues that come up afterward ...and sometimes long afterward. No, I'm not a wedding crasher, I'm married to a rabbi. This, combined with what I've learned about love from my own life, my studies of the ancient teachings of Kabbalah, and counseling couples puts me in a unique position to observe what really goes on in the different stages of a relationship. It forms the basis for what I'd like to share with you in the pages that lie ahead.

My approach to counseling couples is quite different from that of a traditional marriage counselor. I meet couples at various stages of their relationship. They could be dating, or struggling with the pressures of starting a family or trying to rekindle the passion in a relationship that's decades old. When we start working together, I make it clear that they are engaged in a process that is larger than a specific solution. Regardless of the outcome (whether the couple stays together or not), the experience is something their souls need. Relationships can be our biggest source of pain, as well as our biggest source of joy. When couples first come through my door, I often see the former. The love is still there, but they lack the right tools to fix it. With consciousness followed up by action, we can all reclaim the relationship that we want and so richly deserve.

Many times when we come to a difficult place in our lives, when we feel completely blocked, our first instinct is to search for a way out. We lack the perspective to see that every challenge is an opportunity disguised as a dead end.

My message is as simple as this: love isn't something we need to find, accumulate, and protect. There's only one way to receive love, and that's to give it away. *Rethink Love* isn't going to teach you how to have a happy relationship. It's going to provide you with the tools to create a meaningful, purpose-filled relationship.

One where both you and your partner seek to improve not just yourselves, but the world around you. The side effects of which just happen to be joy and fulfillment.

More than a self-help manual, this book encourages you to take responsibility and action, which is the best way to enrich your life and love more deeply. I believe in practical, immediate, long-lasting solutions, but there are no panaceas or quick fixes when it comes to having a successful relationship.

The truth is that every relationship has its problems, and the relationships that work are the relationships we work on.

This book will take you on a journey of self-discovery. I draw from personal experience, as well as from couples I've counseled, current scientific and psychological findings, as well as the teachings of Kabbalah. Kabbalah is time-tested wisdom that explains the complexities of the material and the nonmaterial world, along with the physical and spiritual nature of all humanity. Each chapter contains kabbalistic principles and explores how to apply them to your life and relationships to bring you closer to the intimate, lasting love for which we all long.

For thousands of years, kabbalists have taught that every human being is born with the potential for greatness, and Kabbalah is a remarkably effective means for activating that potential. Kabbalah is a practical tool. Its purpose is to bring clarity, understanding, and freedom to our lives. Applying its principles to your life will be hard work, but then, so is anything worthwhile. According to Kabbalah, you are destined for greatness in every area of your life. This is your birthright, but it's your *responsibility* to pursue the life and the love that you want.

Whereas many self-help approaches show you how to go around an issue, skirt negative feelings, or learn to cope with a situation, Kabbalah takes you through it. Not around, not medicated, but through it to the other side. The goal of Kabbalah is transformation. Kabbalah changes people, which is why it plays such an essential part of my approach. I've seen firsthand how kabbalistic wisdom and real-world solutions can bring Light and strength into even the most challenging situation. Every day I see people applying this approach to their lives and changing for the better.

One thing that's important to establish at the very outset: There is no such thing as a stable marriage. There are happy marriages and unhappy marriages, but not stable ones. In all areas of life, we are either moving forward or falling back, but never staying the same. Embracing this basic truth empowers couples to change their consciousness. When we change our thoughts, we change the very nature of our relationships with ourselves and with our partners.

Everything can be changed because life is constantly changing.

Rethink Love will dispel the many misconceptions you may have about love, and once they're cleared away, this book will help you navigate your relationship through both good and challenging times. And here's my first piece of advice: be wary of relationship advice. (Yes, I see the irony in this, but hear me out.) Be careful who you confide in. If you confide in a person with their own relationship issues, you will likely receive advice that mirrors their struggles. I will be sharing many aspects of my twenty-year marriage: the good, the bad, and the extremely embarrassing (I apologized in advance to my husband, Michael). I hope that this book inspires you to look into your relationships with truth, honesty, and an open heart.

I've written *Rethink Love* in three parts:

- **Part 1: Me** is about the fundamental first and most crucial step in relationships, one that most people miss, the relationship you have with yourself. Don't underestimate the importance of cultivating this. By working on knowing and accepting yourself, you are

15

elevating all the other relationships in your life—in business, family, and love.

- **Part 2: Moving from Me to We** is about how to maintain your beliefs and stay grounded in who you are while navigating the intricacies of a relationship with someone else.

- **Part 3: We** is a manual for growing your relationship to its ultimate potential.

**Now it's time to rethink
what we think we know about love.**

Part One

Me

If anyone has to change
it's probably ~~you~~ me

Chapter One

You Complete You

"Children have never been very good at listening to their elders, but they have never failed to imitate them." [1] **— James Baldwin**

. . . .

Take an in-depth look at your childhood beliefs about love. Let's say you have a spouse who is remote and unaffectionate. When you look more closely at yourself, you might find that quality in one or both of your parents. Perhaps they were cold and unloving towards each other, and thus, that's what you subconsciously model love to be.

I'm not suggesting you blame your parents, but I am proposing that you undertake a clear-eyed investigation into where your ideas about love originated. Examine your earliest model of a loving relationship. Don't judge anyone here, not your parents, not yourself; approach this question with curiosity. Children mimic what they see adults doing; that's only natural, so their behavior mirrors what they observe at home. How has this model affected your current relationship?

We each have a history of life experiences that have shaped us. In part, we are a sum of our past, made up of how we gave love and how we received love, along with the hurts we hold in our hearts, what baggage we've claimed from past relationships, and what movies are in our heads. I want to write, as much as you want to read about improving your relationship with your significant other, but I will always return to the relationship you have with yourself. We all know this is where it begins, but the surprising news is this is also where it ends.

Very often, problems between couples arise not because we are unaware of our partner's story or past, but because we are not aware of the stories in our minds. That's where we have to begin: with me. As Socrates said, *know thyself*. And then, as you'll see in Part 2 of this book, once you know thyself, then you can know thy partner. In truth, it's impossible to maintain an elevated consciousness with another person until you have first delved into—and learned to appreciate—the essence of your own soul.

Many bright people throw themselves wholeheartedly into understanding the world while neglecting the endeavor of understanding themselves. I went to my doctor for my annual check-up. Knowing how much I travel, he asked me if I had any trips coming up. I told him I was preparing to give a lecture on meeting our potential. "Our potential in what?" he asked. "Our potential in life," I responded. He looked at me with a confused expression, and it dawned on me that most people don't think of life in these terms. In our society, we tend to think of our goals, not our potential. Our primary focus is on finding our soulmate, getting married, having children, getting fit, losing weight, saving money for retirement, and on and on. Don't get me wrong. Goals are essential, but we tend to place too much emphasis on them while losing sight of the bigger picture: manifesting our life's purpose. So how do I figure out my purpose? That's a big question!

It starts with introspection and identifying your beliefs. The journey of self-discovery is lifelong, and your purpose is ever-evolving. You can find clues to your unique purpose by contemplating what you enjoy doing and what gives you a sense of satisfaction. Then, extrapolate that by asking yourself how you can share this with the world. Leading a purpose-filled life means taking your gifts and sharing them. It is through this process of lifelong self-discovery that we find true fulfillment.

We are accustomed, as individuals and as a society, to look outward for fulfillment. So begins the tale of every troubled relationship because unless you know and understand yourself, your relationships happen *to* you instead of *through* you.

KABBALISTIC PRINCIPLE:

Every situation in life has an external and an internal aspect, and they are rarely, if ever, the same. Our body and all of its desires represent the external aspect, and our soul represents the internal aspect.

· · · · · · · ·

What you seek can never come from an external place. Not from a job, not from a relationship, not from beauty, or wealth. Not from anything you can see or touch. The deep longing we feel to connect to something larger than ourselves can only be satisfied by exploring our inner aspect. This is our link to what kabbalists call the "Light of the Creator," the "Light," the "Source," and what most call "God." Disconnection from our inner aspect results in feelings of unhappiness, depression, anxiety, emptiness, and a constant need for validation. When we bring our focus back to our inner aspect, we rediscover the happiness and fulfillment for which we long. This is also true in relationships.

The external aspect is expressed as the physical things our partners give us. Conversely, the internal aspect of the relationship is the joy you take in discovering the unique imprint of your partner's soul. When you can connect to their internal aspect, your connection with them will continue regardless of physical hardships or obstacles. You are connected to their soul, which transcends the physical.

I've come to find, in my journey, that being centered in yourself is the foundation of being strong. The more I'm in touch with what's inside me, the more I can do for others. If I'm understanding and compassionate with regard to my own body, thoughts, and emotions, then so too can I be compassionate towards others'. We can't give what we don't have. You can never do all these things for somebody else first and then get to yourself.

It's not easy to create this shift, but it's the only way to create a strong sense of self. I'm not asking you to become self-centered, but instead to be

23

centered on yourself, so you don't become reliant on your partner for that strength. The difference is crucial. I'm not saying to be self-centered; I'm saying to be "centered" and self-interested. It's about being in touch with your inner self—tending, supporting, and strengthening the soul aspect of you.

When we are connected to our internal aspect (the Source), we are not waiting for someone to fulfill us. Love is never outside of ourselves; love is within us.

Becoming Aware is the First Step

Kalonymus Kalman Shapira was an inspiring kabbalist whose work has profoundly affected me. His words are as fresh and relevant as if he'd written them today. His life was taken in the Holocaust.

He buried his journals in the concentration camp where he was being held. In one writing, called *The Student's Obligation,* he posited that a child must be imbued "with a vision of his potential greatness" and be "an active participant in his own development." [2]

Kalman looks at the differences between the soul and the body. The latter represents the tangible world—you can see it, you can feel it, it's what's left behind when you die. But the soul is invisible and intangible. Emotions, thoughts, and feelings are only apparent to the soul, and the starting point for coming to know it is introspection. In Kalman's words, "Each person needs to take an honest evaluation, by honest self-awareness, of the intricacies of his unique soul." [3]

Rethink Moment

- How do you feel when you wake up in the morning, and what excites you?

- What is your intention for each day?

- When you make decisions, what are they based on? Outside influence? Comfort? Or deep self-awareness?

Only you can be true to yourself. No one else can do that for you. This is your work in this lifetime.

Chapter Two

Being True to Yourself

There is a collective mindset in our culture that being romantically loved by someone else will lead to self-acceptance. Like Bridget Jones,[4] we believe that love will give us value that we don't inherently possess: *I must be worthwhile, because after all, he loves me just as I am.* Instead of taking the time to explore who we are and what we want, we embark on a quest to find our perfect match, thinking that's the road to happiness when it's just a disappointing dead-end. It's not reasonable to rely on outside situations to make us happy. However, when it comes to relationships, we fall into the trap of expecting that our partner will make us happy. Because that's what happens when we meet someone. Isn't it?

Many of us feel a strong desire—or sometimes, a desperate need—to find "the one," the romantic partner out there who will make our lives feel complete. We wonder how we'll meet this person, and how we'll keep them once we do. But that feeling we crave can only be found within ourselves. I know with absolute certainty, that unless you have developed a strong relationship with yourself, it will be impossible to sustain a meaningful relationship with someone else, romantic or otherwise. If you set out to get that ring on your finger, to live happily ever after without ever experiencing the vital process of self-exploration, you're building your relationships on a weak foundation.

Look through the online dating apps, and you'll see all the different qualifications that prospective partners need to meet: financial stability, physical attractiveness, and a love of pets are a few of the most common.

When we emphasize the wrong things, be it money or physical attraction, chances are we are going to attract the wrong mate.

We want all these things, and they have importance, but the emphasis needs to be placed on what is lasting. Money gets spent and looks fade. The only thing that lasts is what is on the inside. What's important is that you share a compatible spirituality, moral code, and place value on the same things in life. This ensures that you can grow together and navigate together through life's inevitable challenges.

Unfortunately, for many people who are depressed, or frightened of being alone, companionship can seem like a quick salve. But relationships are never a way out of personal difficulties, emotional or otherwise. The person you love can share in your fulfillment, they can support you as you find your fulfillment, but they cannot provide it.

KABBALISTIC PRINCIPLE:

You Can't Give What You Don't Possess

· · · · · · · ·

People in relationships often end up feeling lost because they've never found themselves in the first place. We expect our spouse to fulfill us and make us feel validated, important, and valued. This is an antiquated way of thinking that was born out of the era in which it was taught that women were nothing if they were not married. This is a recipe for disaster, a state of consciousness that leads only to disappointment, dissatisfaction, anger, stress, and frustration. I have seen countless instances in which one person in the relationship, with the best of intentions, makes the mistake of sacrificing who they are to be half of a couple. The result is a train wreck every time.

Each partner needs to be their own person, only then can you be complete together.

None of us is meant to be half a person, married or single. For love to survive the test of time, we must change our thinking. 1 and 1 make 2. Recently I met my friend Rachel's fiancé, Aaron. I was surprised to learn that they had decided to get married after dating for just six months, and after living in the same city for only three weeks. Furthermore, the wedding was just a few months off. When I asked him some basic questions to get to know him a little better, it became apparent that his bride-to-be was hearing these things for the first time, as well.

Once they got married, they were planning to move to a small town outside the city, although Rachel loved the city and her job there as a yoga instructor. When she expressed some apprehension about small-town life, Aaron pointed out how costly it would be for her to travel regularly into the city. She countered, explaining that she'd spend the money she made from teaching yoga to pay for the travel expenses. As he continued to question her, Rachel blushed and shrank down in her chair. Finally, he said, "I don't want my wife to work. I want her to be waiting for me with dinner ready when I get home."

He may have told her all of this before, and at the moment she thought it was romantic. Now, in the context of not being able to pursue interests outside of the home, it felt like exactly what it was: a controlling gesture that isn't romantic at all.

After he succeeded in bullying her into submission, he then gently rubbed her arm and said, "But you know I love you, and I'll support whatever you want." What she paid attention to were his saccharine words, rather than how she felt when he was questioning her simple desires. This is because she is more connected to external feedback than her own internal feedback. It became painfully clear that they saw the relationship very differently.

I pointed out that perhaps Rachel and Aaron needed to slow things down. Despite their attraction to each other, they seemed to have widely divergent views of their marriage and their roles in it. Subconsciously, she is afraid to show her fiancé who she really is because she hasn't fully accepted herself, and fears that if he knows all of who she is, then he will no longer want her. She wants to be loved and in love because being in love feels good, and that's something she has always craved. But creating a life together has to begin with some basic questions. "Do I know what I want, and can I make myself happy? Can my partner do the same? And how does this look when we put all this together?"

Be true to yourself, because nobody else is going to, nor can they do it for you. This is a necessary step for each individual because if we stop paying attention to who we are and what we believe, then we eventually lose track of who we are. The danger here is that when this happens, other people's thoughts and judgments become our own.

How do We Begin to be True to Ourselves?

Being true to yourself begins with listening to what's going on inside your brain and your body.

There is great strength in being able to trust yourself to make the right choices.

Women, for instance, are brought up to be nurturing caretakers of others, and at some point, girls get the message–from the media, from each other, and their parents–that they need to succeed in every way: academically, professionally, physically, emotionally, and spiritually. And to top it off, are expected to be in perfect balance and total control which is a complete impossibility!

At the same time these impossible expectations are being set for them, they sense from those around them that too much focus on themselves is unseemly. Like the shoemaker whose family goes barefoot, women tend to pour their energy into so many places that they forget to take care of themselves. This can lead to a few detrimental outcomes, especially where our relationships are concerned.

Most of us live our lives in one (or more) of these three states of mind:
- We care too much about what people think.
- We hold our tongues to the point where we can no longer repress our feelings and explode.

- We live in a sea of resentment, which only gets broader and deeper every time we deny ourselves what we want or are unwilling to ask for it.

Small children have no compunctions about saying, even shrieking, what they want. But at a critical point in 3rd, 4th, or 5th grade, the shame of wanting sets in. Having desires and expressing them somehow become impolite and socially unacceptable. That's the message we get: that we should wait until we are offered what we want. Sometimes I look at the rants and raves of small children, and I wish I could say, totally untainted by social norms and preferences, without shame or blame, "I WANT THIS!"

Asking for what we want is uncomfortable at first because it means being vulnerable and having the willingness to allow ourselves to be seen. First, we have to know what we want. Then, we have to believe it's okay to want it and that we are worthy of receiving it. Then, we need to give it to ourselves as best we can and be willing to ask others for it. A pretty tall order! But one that is necessary for our happiness and it gets easier each time.

The teachings of Kabbalah state that desire is the most important gift we receive in this life. Desire is what motivates us, it gives us our drive, and how we use it determines the course of our lives.

It is through examining both what we want and, more importantly, *why* we want it, that we gain the most insight into ourselves and those around us. Many reading a relationship book have a strong desire to improve their current relationship. So strong, that they commit many hours to it.

Sustaining our desire is paramount. Because without the force of desire propelling us forward, we remain stationary. Just as important as knowing what we want and asking for it, is staying hungry and continuously desiring to drive our relationships to higher levels of connectedness, fulfillment, and intimacy.

Releasing the
Shame of Wanting

One afternoon a few years ago, I was on my way out of the house. I had literally just pulled out of the driveway and was on my way to my next appointment. Simultaneously, and unbeknownst to me, my eight-year-old daughter, Miriam, was arriving home from school. Due to the timing, I didn't see her, but she sure saw me.

As I was on a call and then going straight into my next meeting, it wasn't until after the meeting that I noticed I had a voicemail. When I dialed into my voicemail at the other end, I heard a voice filled with hysteria. It was my daughter.

"MOMMY!," she managed to get out through hysterical gasps while trying to catch her breath and speak all at once. "I saw your car as we were driving in and then you just drove off! Did you see me? I was so excited that you were going to be home, there are so many things I wanted to tell you. Were you on your phone?" *Click*—end of message.

I listened to my daughter's message, and I was struck by something. She had called and expressed, in the most pure and simple way, what she had hoped and wanted. She had wanted me to be home, plain and simple. There was no blame nor malice in her message—she just happened to express what she had desired—and it was utterly uncorrupted by shame. It was innocent and true.

In truth, we should feel no shame in wanting things–physically or emotionally—and we should have no shame in asking for what we want. How else will people know what to give us if we don't? Often, wanting something is considered to be a bad thing, but it isn't. It is a quintessentially human desire. It's how we know we're alive.

I spent the first 28 years of my life looking outside myself for answers. I was so caught up in everyone else. "What do they think? What do they want? What can I do for my family, my peers, my fellow students, or my colleagues at work?"

I would have done better to ask myself, "Am I a person who can stand on my own? Do I have enough insight into who I am and what I believe to make the right choices for myself?" These are profound questions that very few of us ever ask ourselves, but should. This greatly impacts relationships, because if you don't know what you believe, then you may choose a partner based on arbitrary things. For instance, you may find someone you like very much, more than you have liked anyone else in previous relationships, but still, aren't entirely sure they are the one. But eventually, you become swayed because your parents and friends are confident that this is the perfect person for you. The next thing you know, you've made a very serious decision based on the thoughts and feelings of others, instead of heeding your inner voice.

"Raise yourself above the crowd, bring out what makes you unique. Become a person who can choose for himself." [5]
– Kalonymous Kalman Shapira

If you're nobody on your own, then you are nobody in a group and if the group is gone, then so are you. Most have been conditioned on our views of the world by our families, and heavily influenced by peer groups during the formative years of our lives. It's easy to think along the paths of others. Instead, actively swim upstream, struggling against the flow to find yourself and connect to your soul.

So, how do we do this?

We must first be willing to let go of who we thought we should be in order to be who we really are. This is the process of first meeting and then embracing our true selves. Only then are we able to stand whole, steadfast in what we believe, even if our beliefs are not accepted or valued by others.

Create Your Credo

Who we are and the beliefs we have settled upon come from a series of experiences and choices we have made consciously or subconsciously throughout our lives. Beliefs are choices, and no one but you has the authority over your personal beliefs. Your beliefs are in jeopardy only when you don't know what they are. What beliefs have brought you to the place where you are today? I read *This I Believe: The Personal Philosophies of Remarkable Men and Women,* edited by Jay Allison and Dan Gediman.[6] These essays focus not only on what can be learned at the moment, but over a lifetime. A credo is a powerful tool to help you become more aware of what you believe. Writing out your credo will help you align your decisions going forward with your authentic self. It will also help you appreciate where you have come from and how much you've already accomplished.

Here is an exercise from *This I Believe* that I recommend.[7]

Write your credo:

1. **Tell a story about you:** Be specific. Take your belief out of the ether and ground it in the events that have shaped your core values. Consider moments when this belief was formed or tested or changed. Think of your own experience, work, and family, and write down the things you know that no one else does. Your story need not be heart-warming nor gut-wrenching—it could be funny—but it should be real.

2. **Be brief:** Your statement should be between 500 and 600 words.

3. **Name your belief:** If you can't name it in a sentence or two, your essay might not be about belief. Also, rather than writing a list, consider focusing on one core belief.

4. **Be positive:** Write about what you do believe, not what you don't.

5. **Be personal:** Make your essay about you; use the first person. Tell a story from your own life.

I arrived at my credo in the months immediately following the birth of my second son, Josh. Because initially, I struggled with accepting his diagnosis of Down syndrome, it became clear to me that I needed to stop and look at my belief system. I discovered that not only did I not like some of my views, but many of them were not really mine. They were opinions formed over my lifetime, some of which had been pressed upon me by other people, while others derived directly from my fears. Josh's diagnosis and my anxieties about it made me stop and ask myself, "What do I choose to believe?" As a result, I came up with my credo: "In change, there is great power."

Among the many conflicting emotions I felt in those tumultuous days after Josh's birth were a sense of betrayal by my body, distance from my husband, and separation from my first child. The injustice of hearing a list of limitations the doctors said Josh would have—things he would never say, do, or experience—made me feel like he had no future at all. I realized I was a person invested in others' opinions of me. I would read people's faces that I passed, staring at me and my newborn, wondering what they saw, wondering if they pitied me, if they could tell he was different?

It was an incredibly painful time, but as I've learned since, such times contain a huge opportunity. Instead of letting this experience define me, I chose change. I chose to embrace my son and discover the beauty of his soul and all he could offer. I chose change.

In change, there is great power.

I chose to persevere regardless of the present circumstance because I have come to know that strong people are committed to change and growth every day of their lives. They live their lives with values, passion, and dreams even when others may not acknowledge, affirm, or agree with them. I know that in change there is great power

Each one of us is deserving of greatness. My husband always says, "Greatness is not reserved for the great; the great are those who have risen to meet their destiny." [8] Being who we are, and living our lives with truth and honesty is part of that destiny. Be you. Be disciplined in your pursuit.

Chapter Three

Be Your Own Mr. or Ms. Right

"Be yourself, everyone else is already taken."
— Oscar Wilde [9]

. . . .

As we step into our true selves, I have noticed an interesting hiccup that sometimes arises. Let's say you set a new goal to write a screenplay. You feel lit up by your ideas and feel impassioned as you work. Then you're sitting in a movie theatre, and you watch a trailer for a shockingly similar film. Suddenly, you are freaking out. You might be feeling like you've missed your chance, or like your idea isn't original, or that no one will be interested now. What once was a creative endeavor that brought you excitement and bliss, now feels pointless and dreary. But wait!

This is where your authenticity comes in. By bringing your unique self into your projects, relationships, and life at large, you are creating something valuable.

KABBALISTIC PRINCIPLE:

Every single one of us is destined for greatness: we each have unique gifts and talents given to us so we can impact the world in a way that no one else can.

. . . .

Think of it this way. Anyone could walk into a bookstore and buy a cookbook by a famous chef that contains a specific recipe. Thousands of people could buy the same ingredients, follow the recipe, and create the same delicious dish. But each time it will taste a little different, possibly *very* different. In some instances it will be glorious, Michelin Star Award winning. (If I made it, you probably wouldn't ask for seconds. Dessert though is a different story.) The point is this: YOU are what makes your creation special. And the more of your unique, authentic, singular self you bring to everything you do, the more those efforts are going to shine. Not only that, they will bring you great joy, as well, creating blessings in every direction.

So what does it mean to be authentic? Most people think it means to be honest, which are certainly related, but it really means to be genuine, and therefore entitled to acceptance. I find that last part key: entitled to acceptance. Being authentic is an acknowledgment that we are imperfect, yet still worthy of belonging. My hope for all of us is that we come to know that who we are is enough. Somewhere along the way, we learned not to love ourselves. The good news: this can be unlearned. If we wait until we become "perfect" before we love ourselves—until we're thin enough, successful enough, or happy enough—we will be waiting forever.

Psychologist David Schnarch puts it this way. "It's challenging to become an authentic adult because it means, among other things, soothing your own bad feelings without the help of another, pursuing your own goals, and standing on your own two feet. Most people associate these skills with singlehood, but marriages cannot succeed unless we claim our sense of self in the presence of another." [10]

Belonging vs. Fitting In: Standing on My Own

In high school, I was what most would consider popular. I fit in. I spoke, behaved and dressed by the unspoken standards of the popular crowd. I later realized that I repressed who I was in the face of any threat of not being accepted. I wasn't being truthful about my passions or interests, nor did I divulge any weakness or fears. This required so much effort that it didn't leave much time or energy to explore who I actually was, to ask myself if I was happy, or to spend time on things I found to be meaningful. I stopped asking myself who I wanted to be, out of fear of being ostracized. Fitting in is not belonging! Fitting in often requires that you change or suppress your authentic self in order to emulate others. Belonging, on the other hand, is arriving on your own terms, with your unique voice and style. Belonging is being accepted for who you are, with the knowledge that even your worst character traits or flaws will not be used against you to inflict pain. It's not a realistic notion to believe that all people will accept us. Others may attack you, but if you accept yourself, then you'll be able to move past those times without shaking your self-worth.

There is an old Yiddish word, echt, which means "to be true, to be genuine, to be authentic." To truly belong, you have to be echt. How can we be accepted by others in a meaningful and genuine way if we don't love and accept who we are at our core? How can we speak and act and think in perfect accord with our core self, if on some level we don't like who we are?

This kind of authenticity and self-acceptance is the baseline, the foundation upon which happy lives are built. Without authenticity, our relationships lack fulfillment, intimacy, and happiness. Sometimes people don't live authentic lives before they start a relationship, which can be challenging because, throughout our lives, we go through a process of self-discovery. As we go further along on this journey, we may find ourselves with someone who doesn't accept us.

The most worthwhile thing we can do is be ourselves—our best selves. Be your own Mr. or Ms. Right. Living each moment with authenticity requires constant effort, but ultimately it's more exhausting to deny who we are and live someone else's truth.

Professor and bestselling author Dr. Brené Brown has a great tip for maintaining your sense of self even in the face of criticism. Take a 1x1 inch piece of paper and write down the name of every person who has your best interests at heart. Next time someone criticizes you, if their name isn't on your list, by all means, be open to what they have to say, but don't allow yourself to be derailed by their opinions. [11]

True Validation
Comes from You

By definition, to validate means to prove that something is based on truth or fact. When we seek validation from others, we are looking for acceptance, to prove that we are "okay." Seeking validation derives from insecurity and self-doubt. Feedback, on the other hand, is simply information. It's a response to what we're doing, and as such, it can be very useful. In a nutshell, when you're looking for validation, you're saying, in effect, "help make me okay." When you're asking for feedback, you're saying, in effect, "help make me better."

Seeking validation from your partner can be especially problematic. For instance, if your partner validates you by saying you're attractive, and this is something you've never believed about yourself, then this belief is now based entirely on his or her opinion. Even more regrettable, if they change their opinion of you, then you no longer feel attractive, because you never did in the first place. See the rub? Unless you acknowledge and accept the things that make you wonderful inside and out, you are going to be wholly reliant on outside validation.

Invalidation is a pattern in which one partner subtly or directly puts down the thoughts, feelings, or character of the other. Sometimes invalidation may not actually be taking place, but it feels like it when you're constantly looking to someone else to make you feel complete and valued. A couple I counseled was dealing with this very issue. When they first got together, the wife was the more professionally successful of the two. Eventually, they had three children, at which point she decided to quit her job to spend more time with them. As time went on, she found herself feeling increasingly emotionally demanding around her husband. And the needier she felt, the less into her he seemed to be.

For a while, the wife blamed her husband for pulling away from her. Luckily, she figured out what was really going on. Because she was no longer working, she lost an essential part of herself and began looking to her husband to provide a part of her identity that was lost. Once she realized this, she began working full-time again, juggling her career while also raising

40

her children and her husband once again became very present. She didn't tell him to change or to be interested in her. Rather, she placed emphasis on her own actions, pursued what she desired, and stopped waiting for him to give her validation.

Rethink Moment

In taking the steps towards validating yourself, here are a few questions to ask:

• **In the past, what aspect of yourself have you looked to someone else to validate?**

• **What are your current expectations from your partner?**

• **Understanding that validation can only come from you, how can you provide yourself with the validation you've been seeking from your partner?**

With this awareness, you can begin to take the pressure off your relationship as your sole source of happiness. Taking responsibility for your happiness enables you to have a sense of purpose. As a result, your partner will start to treat you differently simply because you've shifted your own energy. It works just like that.

If you are single, this process of making yourself whole also helps you to attract the kind of mate that will lead to a fulfilling relationship. This time is your opportunity to get to know yourself better and to love yourself more deeply. Feeling uncomfortable in your own skin is like having a wet bathing suit on for too long. Feeling insecure about your opinions and not knowing what choices to make is like having sand in that wet bathing suit. Just like the wet, sandy bathing suit, the insecurities and discomfort can be taken off and washed away.

Most people spend a big part of their life not liking the person staring back at them in the mirror, which is problematic because the longest and most important relationship you will ever have is the one you have with yourself. The bottom line is that happiness comes from within, not from someone or somewhere else. This might read like a truism, but as the kabbalist, Rav Moshe Chaim Luzzatto said, "The greatest teachings are not the ones we haven't learned, but practicing the ones we already know."

Chapter Four

Love and Little Changes

"For the past 33 years, I have looked in the mirror every morning and asked myself, 'If today were the last day of my life, would I want to do what I am about to do today?' And whenever the answer has been 'no' for too many days in a row, I know I need to change something." — Steve Jobs [12]

. . . .

I want to share with you the story of Peter and Sara. Although Sara married a wonderful man, she found herself dissatisfied. Throughout their nine-year union, she was able to see the good in Peter less and less, while becoming hyper-focused on the things about him that bothered her. At this point, it was a pretty long list, which included the way he ate his food, his slovenly ways, even the way he brushed his teeth—when he did, that is. High on her list of annoyances was the way he washed his hands—getting water all over the bathroom counter. It looked like a duck had been splashing around in the basin! When she leaned over the sink to put on her eyeliner, she'd find her blouse soaked in water. Peter wasn't Sara's only source of dissatisfaction. She felt depressed and disappointed in general with a life that seemed to include no excitement, no passion. But her marriage remained the primary sticking point. When things reached their breaking point, Sara would confront Peter with the many things he needed to change to make their marriage work. The only time she felt badly about her litany of grievances was when Peter's chronic Crohn's disease would flare up.

Then one day, following a surgical procedure to mitigate his symptoms, Peter unexpectedly died. Sara was left alone with her list of grievances

43

and plenty of time to think about everything that had bothered her. From her new perspective, with Peter suddenly gone from her life forever, Sara saw that none of her complaints were genuinely significant. She realized that marriage isn't about her needs or their needs, or even how well they communicate their needs; it's about loving and being loved. Marriage is about loving another person and receiving love in return.

Kabbalists believe the universe reflects our lives back to us. Our first reaction is to think it's the other person's fault. Kabbalah teaches us that whenever we have a strong adverse reaction to a quality we see in another person — whether it's selfishness, or insincerity, or bossiness — we're being given a strong hint about where we need to focus our attention to foster *our* growth. Put simply, what we don't like in others is what we need to change within ourselves. If you find someone selfish, take a look at how you can be more selfless. If you see insincerity, evaluate your sincerity. Often we have a mistaken belief that if our partner would just change, our relationship would be better. I challenge you to reevaluate your beliefs — rethink them.

At times you will feel that your partner must be deliberately trying to unhinge you; after all, no one has ever made you this frustrated or angry! But actually, the frustration is a sign, a flare illuminating what you most need to change, and it shows up even in the healthiest relationships. What bothers you most about your mate has little or nothing to do with that person. Instead, it has everything to do with how you feel about yourself. Think about your partner and focus on something that bothers you about them. Now ask yourself: Where am I also like this? When do I behave this way? If you see your partner as a nag, or defensive, or unsupportive, ask yourself if it's possible that you might be bringing that quality to your relationship.

The truth is that what bothers us most about our mate has everything to do with how we feel about ourselves. That ideal person you've been trying so hard to find or to turn your partner into simply doesn't exist. So don't waste your life in search of a unicorn. Instead, become the best version of yourself you can be.

This brings me to a core principle:

if anybody has to change, it's me.

It's not our job to change other people (and that's a hopeless task anyway.) The change we need to see lies within ourselves. Once you've made this shift in your awareness, you'll find that all those little things that used to bother you so much suddenly don't affect you anymore.

KABBALISTIC PRINCIPLE:

A person's potential is revealed by their actions.

· · · · · · · ·

Now the question becomes what kind of person you want to be, and how you can use your relationship as a mirror to help you.

We all want to make changes in order to improve the quality of our relationships and expand the breadth of our experiences. Any change we wish to see in our life begins with a change we make within ourselves. Knowing this, we establish the goal, visualize what we want, and develop a clear understanding of the steps necessary to achieve our goals. And then nothing. Why not? You understood why you want the change. You made the to-do list. The only thing standing between you and your desired experience is you, along with your inherent aversion to change, of course.

I'm sure you're thinking, "Wait! I don't hate change! I *want* things in my relationship to improve." It's one thing to want change and another to *pursue* it. Like everything in life, change begins with a thought, a belief, or an idea. It starts with a shift in your outlook.

Start with Changing How You Feel About Change

Rethink Moment

What do you want to change?

- **Find love or renew love**

- **Pursue a new career**

- **Get a promotion**

- **Lose weight**

- **Start a family**

- **Write a book**

- **Get a degree**

- **Start an exercise regimen**

- **Stay in better touch with your friends**

- **Stop smoking**

All of these lofty goals are attainable, and they all begin with changing your consciousness and then aligning that new perspective with new actions. Kabbalist Rav Berg, my father-in-law, was once quoted as saying, "Kabbalah isn't easy, but it's simple." This applies perfectly to change. It is incredibly simple and yet so difficult to implement. But why?

New = Bad

Aversion to change is deep-seated in human nature. A 2010 study conducted at the University of Arkansas found that people overwhelmingly found older objects or established behaviors preferable to new ones. [13] In a blind taste test, one group was told the chocolate they were about to sample had been produced for three years, whereas the other group was told their chocolate had been produced for seventy-three years. The second group rated their chocolate overwhelmingly much higher than the group who thought the recipe was newer, even though the chocolate was precisely the same. We have a built-in rating system that says new (change) = bad. This is one of the reasons people stay in unhappy marriages for so long. It may be unfulfilling and even painful, but it's familiar, and that's comforting. Something new is usually uncomfortable at first.

What if Change Leads to a Situation that is Worse?

Another reason that people don't make changes is the fear that they may end up worse off. Better the devil you know than the one you don't, as the saying goes. I know an overweight couple that describes themselves as happily married. However, several times a year, he decides to go on a diet. At first, he's highly motivated and disciplined, but just as he starts to see results, his wife becomes difficult. I don't know how aware they are of the cause and effect, but seeing her husband start to change makes the wife very uncomfortable. As a result, she begins to act in ways that are atypical of her character. This tension in their relationship is the catalyst for him abandoning his diet, and as the pounds add back on, their relationship returns to the status quo.

This case is hardly unique. Lots of us avoid making changes we deeply desire because those changes might upset the careful balance of our relationships. Change is uncomfortable, not just for the person initiating the new behavior, but for those close to them, as well. People don't really want their significant other to change for many different reasons. Some become resentful and jealous and worry they may no longer have a central role in their partner's life. Others believe the change will affect their partner in some fundamental way that they might not like. In essence, we fear not only the discomfort of change itself, but also the effect it may have on those we love. It's fear on two levels!

Little by Little

"It's funny how things change slowly until the day we realize that they've changed completely." — Nancy Gibbs [14]

Change isn't something that needs to be overwhelming if you actively pursue change in little ways every day. This brings me to the idea of trim tabs, invented by philosopher and engineer Buckminster Fuller. [15] Trim tabs are the tiny rudders built into larger rudders on seagoing ships or passenger planes. Fuller understood that if such large vessels were to change direction suddenly, the pressure on a single rudder might cause it to snap. So he came up with trim tabs as a solution. "Just moving the little trim tab builds a low pressure that pulls that rudder around," Fuller said. "It takes almost no effort at all." Now even a massive aircraft carrier could change directions with a series of small adjustments. To paraphrase Fuller, we don't have to make huge changes, just small change after small change, which eventually amounts to great change.

One husband in a couple I counsel has some particular ideas about how love should be expressed. In a conversation, he stated, "The only reason we've been so happy lately is because I've let things go." But there's one issue he couldn't let go. He believes that cooking is the way his wife should demonstrate her love for him. More than that, she should also find great satisfaction, happiness, and fulfillment in doing so. So in this world view, an undercooked soup is proof that her love for him is lacking. Needless to say, he is setting himself up for unhappiness. Undercooked soup happens! And I'm not inclined to believe it's related to any lack of love.

Applying a simple trim tab to this scenario, I suggested that instead of brooding in the other room while she put the soup back on, he could have sat in the kitchen and talked with her. He could have used that time to reconnect with her after a long day. The change I encouraged him to make was to recognize her efforts, to focus not on what may have gone wrong in the kitchen, but on the things that went right, and on the time and care that she put into the menu, shopping, and preparation. The love was in the effort, not the outcome.

Gandhi put it this way: "As human beings, our greatness lies not so much in being able to remake the world as in being able to remake ourselves." [16]

Three Tools to Create Change

1. Shift Your Outlook

Your outlook dictates your reality. Your consciousness invites situations, experiences, and people into your life. The voice in your head governs your outlook. If we are honest, we can admit that more often than not, that voice focuses on not only pointing out our shortcomings and flaws, but those of other people.

Your outlook is always a matter of choice. As the Baal Shem Tov, the great 18th-century sage put it, "We think we are sad because things don't go our way when in reality things don't go our way because we are sad."

Jeanne Calment was a living testament to this idea. She lived from 1875-1997. An active tennis player and swimmer, Jeanne Calment took up fencing at 85 and rode her bike until 100. She also had the unhealthy habit of smoking, which she did until she was 117. She died at 122 and credited her longevity to olive oil, port wine, and two pounds of chocolate a week.[17] Research on robust centenarians shows that good habits and genetics certainly contribute to their wellbeing, but a positive outlook on life is high on the list of qualities they share. [18]

It makes sense to say that a thought (negative or positive), a feeling (happy or sad) or an outlook (pessimistic or optimistic) will correspond to what happens to us. Similarly, what happens to us corresponds to our outlook. So, too, your outlook dictates the kind of relationship you are going to have. Your outlook is a guide for behavior and sets expectations for your relationship. The way you think about your life, in fact, changes how you live your life. The way you think about your relationship changes how you express yourself in the relationship. What you think you deserve affects what comes to you.

2. Be Specific
- I'm going to start working out again.
- I'm going to be a more attentive partner.
- I'm going to have more fun with my kids.

Terrific! But now get specific. If you want to start working out again, how about today? And at what time? No change occurs without investing the time and energy needed to focus on the details. To be a more attentive partner, commit to turning off your phone for two hours every night to allow for meaningful conversations with your partner. Talk to your children about what they'd enjoy most, and schedule an activity when you know you'll be fully present. Ambiguous goals usually lead to ambiguous results. Specific goals become attainable.

3. The Commit to a 40-Day-Change Challenge
The number 40 has special spiritual significance in Kabbalah. The most important source of kabbalistic wisdom, The Zohar, explains that it takes 40 days to form a habit or to change a pattern. For instance, if a person born with a stubborn nature does the opposite of what comes naturally for forty days, he will realign his natural tendency. Part of our job in this lifetime is to change our nature, so if we commit to this process, the Creator will assist us in achieving that goal. In forty days (560 hours), you can change whatever you choose. A habit becomes the power that governs you. Commit to taking at least one action towards whatever it is you want for 40 consecutive days. I posed this challenge to the husband for whom the undercooked soup was so important. He decided that for forty days, he wouldn't say anything negative about his wife's cooking. He would offer compliments or nothing at all. To his credit, he met the forty-day challenge, and I'm happy to report that their relationship transformed. In a dramatic shift, appreciation emerged as a primary force in the daily dynamic between husband and wife.

Whatever you look for is what you are going to find.

By training himself to look for the good in the kitchen, he found it in other areas aspects of his life, as well. This created a significant shift in their relationship.

As we've seen, change happens. There's nothing you can do to *keep it* from happening.

Are you actively pursuing change, or are you waiting for it to happen on its own? You must be an active participant. Take the forty-day challenge. And don't fall into the trap of mistaking talk for action. If you intend to be a more supportive partner, imagine how your relationship will transform if, for 40 days, you commit to daily acts of support and kindness. As the old saying goes, "Change occurs when the pain of remaining the same is greater than the pain of changing." [19] But why wait that long? Save yourself a lot of unhappiness and get to work, making that change right now.

Chapter Five

Tikkune: Your Own Personal Baggage Claim

We live in a disposable society. In today's world, there are a lot of quick fixes. If something breaks, just replace it. Don't like your nose? Don't worry—we can fix that! While you can apply this approach to many aspects of your life, it would be foolish to apply this to matters of the heart. When dealing with human emotions, there are no quick fixes. Sometimes people who have been in a dissatisfying relationship for a long time get so frustrated that they decide the only solution is to start anew with someone else. Before you take a drastic step like that, remember that your baggage comes along for the ride; there's no leaving it behind. You're going to keep attracting the same kind of partner until you work through something kabbalists call your *tikkune*.

Tikkune translates as "correction" or "repair." We all carry baggage that has been created not only in this life, but in the lifetimes that came before. I am pragmatic, a linear thinker, and am known as the level-headed one among my peers. And yet, I agree with the kabbalists, who believe our experiences affect our souls lifetime after lifetime, and whatever we have done in past incarnations affects us in future incarnations. Every time we do something negative, we create negative energy that will, at some point, come back into our life—whether it's in this incarnation or the next. Kabbalists call this the law of cause and effect, which is similar to one of the basic principles of Newtonian physics—that for every action there is an equal and opposite reaction. "The law of tikkune decrees that for every action there must be an equal and corresponding reaction—so that ultimately we all receive exactly what we have "asked for," stated Rav Berg. [20]

Every soul that comes into this world has a job to do, which is the spiritual work of correcting a particular quality or trait; this repair is the larger role of tikkune. Tikkune can be helpful in understanding our purpose in the larger context of what our souls are striving to accomplish over many lifetimes. Although life feels random at times, you and I did not appear in this world by chance; we chose our present incarnation as a vehicle for completing our tikkune. Who we are and where we are in life is our responsibility. It means that you alone are the cause of who you are. You have not come about through a process of random selection.

In the tikkune process, there is no such thing as punishment. We cannot escape the effect of past actions, but we can change the severity of the impact based on what we do now, by seeing challenges as opportunities and using them to transform and grow. Recognizing our individual tikkune can spur us to make better choices in our relationships.

Tikkune comes out in many ways, unique to each individual. Your challenges are what bring about your opportunity for transformation. The process of discovering your tikkune is often a painful one, but in actuality, these situations are invitations to work on the areas we most need to address.

Relationships are the best way to identify and work on our tikkune, because they serve as mirrors for who we are. According to Kabbalah, marriage is an ideal opportunity for two individuals to work through their tikkune and advance spiritually. As Rav Berg said, "No marriage is a result of chance, and none is begun on a clean slate. Every marriage is an episode in a series of stories begun long ago, in previous lives." For example, if your tikkune is about commitment, you may subconsciously choose unavailable partners time and time again because you are afraid of what it would mean to be in a long-term relationship. Finding somebody who is available and committing to them would help you greatly in your transformation…not to mention the happiness that it would create in your life.

Your tikkune is not about your husband who betrayed you, your friend who backstabbed you, or your child wearing your patience thin. Regardless of who or what you deem as the cause of your challenges, the opportunity is there to teach you and to become the person you are destined to become.

The natural response when somebody, especially your spouse, hurts you is to lash out. The kabbalistic response is to understand that this is part of your tikkune. Living through this moment in this way is a necessary step in your evolution, which means it's part of a spiritual framework created to help you, not punish you. In this way, every situation that challenges you or brings discomfort bears a gift.

Recently I worked with a student on her tikkune as it related to her marriage. Initially, we thought Ava's tikkune was connected to avoiding confrontation and not wanting to hurt her husband's feelings. An unwillingness to advocate for herself was undoubtedly part of Ava's tikkune, which had played out in many of her personal and professional relationships. She has been married for twenty years, and although dissatisfied for a long time, she stayed because family meant everything to Ava. When she finally told her husband about her dissatisfaction with the marriage, he shut her down.

Ultimately, the question of whether she should leave him or not was secondary, because she realized that the marriage was giving her an opportunity to correct her tikkune. After much introspection, she realized she didn't speak up because of her deep fear of dying alone—a fear that stems not only from this lifetime, but from previous ones. Identifying her tikkune helped Ava move forward in her marriage. She realized that for all his faults, her husband loved her unconditionally and would never leave her. Now she felt freer to confront him over things that annoyed her. When she did speak up, though difficult at first, Ava felt encouraged when her husband eventually began to respond positively.

Discovering our tikkune helps put things in perspective in our lives, and our relationships. If we aren't aware of the importance of tikkune in relationships, then the moment something doesn't go right, we can too easily fall into the mindset, "This just isn't working." Knowing that we're here to work on a particular issue and that we can't run from it, because it will keep showing up in lifetime after lifetime until it's addressed, keeps us aware of the bigger picture.

Working Through
Your Tikkune

How do we effectively work through our tikkune? This can feel daunting, especially because tikkune relates directly to those areas of our life that are the most painful. For the person whose tikkune revolves around commitment, making a commitment is going to bring them face-to-face with great responsibility that at first will seem forced. For the person whose tikkune falls in the area of confrontation, facing their tikkune is going to bring dread and worry.

Whenever you have an unusually intense reaction to a particular situation or notice a pattern of counterproductive behavior (like consistently dating a certain kind of person despite knowing they're not right for you), recognize that it's your tikkune making its presence felt. And remember that it's here to help you by pointing out where you need to focus your attention. This is the first step. Bringing awareness to your tikkune allows you to tell yourself, "I'm not happy about what happened, but I know it's what I need." By making the shift in your perspective, you have already begun the process of addressing your tikkune.

The second step is to come to love this opportunity. Once you've arrived at the deeper level of seeing a challenge as an opportunity, you can work on curbing your impulsive reaction. You've heard the adage about turning the other cheek. If a person hits you, in that moment of pain, anger, shame, and hurt, a kabbalist's advice would be to let go of those emotions. By doing so, the negative things that you may have done to others will be washed away from you, as well.

If this seems a little far-fetched, look at it another way. Let's assume for a moment that your tikkune centers around rejection. To address it, you must confront the feelings that arise from being rejected. Imagine you asked someone out on a date and were turned down. You may then experience feelings of unworthiness, disappointment, and rejection.

The unconscious/ego-mind will react in one of two ways:
- "That person is terrible, and I hate them!"
- "I am worthless. I should just give up."

Over time you'll become more skillful at separating your feelings from the situation. You may never come to love the feeling of being rejected, but you'll begin to see that the feelings that arise don't reflect negatively on who you are. There is great comfort to be found in that. They are simply remnants of your tikkune asking you to greet them with awareness so they can be repaired and released.

KABBALISTIC PRINCIPLE:

When you are open to the big picture, you discover that the process is the purpose. (Everything is for good even if it's not apparent in the moment.)

. . . .

The Process is the Purpose

Too often, people check out too quickly in relationships in the face of their tikkune. Think about it. What if some of the best books, memoirs, or movies ended in the middle of a hardship? Would we feel inspired? Of course not. When we put so much energy and effort into a relationship, it is illogical not to see it through. It doesn't necessarily mean you have to stay, but it does mean you should finish the process.

In the first relationship we read about in the Bible, Eve is created for Adam, and the Bible says, "I will make him a helpmate, to oppose him." From the very first, our mate was intended to support us, but more importantly, to challenge us, push us to grow, and oppose us. In a healthy relationship, you point things out for each other's benefit, even though it may not be what the other person wants to hear. This is how you keep growing together. When you're met with opposition, instead of being quick to conclude that you chose the wrong partner and deserve something better, embrace the process. Remembering there are no accidents in life, appreciate that your partner is the perfect vehicle for your correction. We are given exactly the right partner to help us grow and overcome our tikkune. How long it takes is up to us.

The fact that your partner, or anyone for that matter, triggers you is a sign that this is an opportunity for you to change an aspect of yourself. Change is sparked by discomfort. If you are agitated day in and day out, if you walk away with the same negative thought or emotion or discontentment, then it is an indication of something that needs to change. With this understanding, it will be easier to recognize the trigger because it is a disruption that occurs over and over.

Kabbalists have long taught that we're supposed to leave this world a better place than it was when we came into it. We do this by becoming kinder, more thoughtful, more selfless, and more generous, both in word and deed. Even when considering great spiritual giants, they didn't start as the inspiring leaders they became. Through their unending care of others, their thoughtfulness, and their deep compassion, they became beacons of inspiration to the world. To reach these heights and connect in a meaningful way with those around us, we have to be genuinely open and welcoming to anyone who points out an area of our behavior that needs improvement.

Think of your Tikkune as spinach in your teeth. When you realize you've gone an entire day with a piece of spinach stuck in your teeth, you wonder, "Why didn't anyone tell me?!" Had someone pointed it out, you would have been grateful because then you could have done something about it. Tikkune works the same way. A person striving to meet their potential finds a way to take constructive criticism from the person closest to them, their partner, and use this feedback, however painful, to become the best version of themselves that they can be.

Chapter Six

Thoughts Create Reality

KABBALISTIC PRINCIPLE:

Behavior is born of consciousness;
we are the sum of our thoughts.

. . . .

Everything we manifest begins with a thought. What directs our thoughts is either the desire of our ego or the desire of our soul. But let's back up a bit. What is a soul? Kabbalistically, the soul is potential. Just as a small seed holds the giant potential of an oak, our soul has great potential, as well. It is our responsibility to advance the soul during its journey through this lifetime. So, how do we do this?

We need to envision ourselves like a slab of clay, filled with unmet potential and the ability to mold ourselves into what we want to become. A slab of clay doesn't manifest into something until a sculptor's hands form it. Our actions, words, and thoughts sculpt the energy of our desire, giving it shape, form, and dimension in our reality. For example, when people ruminate negatively about their relationships and how unbearable their partners are, those thoughts are shaping their reality. Those are the seeds that are planted. Though this seems like this only pertains to your individual growth, this concerns your relationships, as well. Every action, word, and thought reveals a part of your soul.

When I speak positively about my partner, I take unmanifested Light from my soul and reveal it in a positive way. I create happiness and joy for myself and him. Conversely, if I speak badly about my partner, I have still revealed a part of my soul, but this time I've created discord and negativity for myself and my partner. Because the soul is potential, every word manifests a part of that potential, and the parts of your soul that you manifest are what you become. If I choose to connect to darkness, then that is what I experience. If I choose to connect to the Light, that is what I will continue to create.

The Ari, a great master of Kabbalah, described the soul as having four levels.

The lowest is called *Nefesh* ("living being"). *Nefesh* is the power that enables us to take action. Every time we move, we are taking a spark of Light from *nefesh* and revealing it in this world through that action. Let's say you walk into your living room, and you see an empty, dirty dish. You have a choice to leave it or take it to the kitchen. Over time, these small decisions accumulate and influence not only your soul but the quality of your relationship.

The second level of the soul is *Ruach* ("spirit"). This force makes speech possible and lends words their power. When we speak positively or negatively, we take Light from this second level of our soul and reveal it accordingly. It can be all too easy in the heat of the moment to say things we'll regret. Any word we use against our partner when we get enraged damages not only our relationships, but also our souls.

The third level is called *Neshama*, ("soul"), which relates to our less complex, everyday thoughts. Every time we think we take a spark from the level of neshama and make it manifest in the world. Much the way we need to train ourselves to watch our actions and words, we need to take great care in what thoughts we dwell on.

The fourth level of the soul is *Chayah*, ("life") which is a higher level of thinking—the source of contemplative thoughts, meditative thoughts, mantras, critical thinking, and all the ways we use our minds to learn and discover.

Every thought has a precursor. In the *Sefer Yetzirah* (*"Book of Formation"*) Abraham writes that before every thought there is a *hirhur,* a pre-thought, a sort of fleeting thought that crosses your mind unbidden, as opposed to more profound thoughts that we spend time and energy to cultivate. Left to their own devices, pre-thoughts tend to veer towards the negative.

- *"I feel fat."*
- *"I hate that person."*
- *"I never get what I want."*
- *"I'm so ashamed."*
- *"How could she do that to me?"*
- *"Why is this happening?"*
- *"I don't deserve this!"*

We also direct these unbidden thoughts at others in the form of judgments.

- *"Her house is a pigsty!"*
- *"He loves the sound of his own voice."*
- *"I can't stand the way he talks to people."*

Pre-thoughts seem harmless enough at first. Most of us can quickly dispel them and get our minds back on track. But when a thought recurs with high frequency, it has an insidious way of becoming part of who we are, leading to such feelings as helplessness, sadness, or self-doubt.

Imagine a married man has fleeting thoughts of attraction for other women. This may seem harmless enough. But over time, he may become more comfortable with these thoughts, and find himself actively flirting with other women. So, what's the problem with that? He's committed to his wife, and flirting is harmless. But is it really? Flirting will most certainly open the door to a flood of other fleeting thoughts of temptation, and what happens when he becomes comfortable with those? The more time you spend thinking about anything, the more you are investing in it. Thoughts are crafty!

Greeting the Stranger

Michelle would get debilitating migraines, especially on Fridays after work. She lived like this for quite some time, until it became too difficult; her body was creating a situation so painful that she'd end up spending the entire weekend in bed. The question was, why? Kabbalists teach us that there is no separation between the body and the mind. According to Rav Berg, disease (or dis-ease) demonstrates a lack of harmony between the soul and the body. If we continually, day after day, year after year, fail to acknowledge our true self and our basic desires and needs, then over time that lack manifests in the body.

Michelle, through a process of discussion and self-reflection, realized that because she wasn't satisfied with her relationship, she would manifest headaches on Fridays, the onset of the weekend, when she and her boyfriend spent the most time together. Even though she didn't feel satisfied in the relationship, she believed she should be appreciative for having a boyfriend, when so many people were looking for one and couldn't find love. She held the belief that "I don't really deserve to be happy, so I don't deserve a better relationship."

Michelle had a very controlling mother who always told her she would be lucky to even find a man who would stick around. Michelle's father had left when she was born.

Michelle recognized that the voice in her head was speaking for her mother about ideas Michelle had been too young to question when she'd first heard them. Michelle came up with a plan and began turning down the volume. Eventually, another voice emerged—the voice of her true essence that craved happiness and love. Whenever Michelle heard that voice, she would greet it with willingness and acceptance. Thereby she was able to change her thoughts and exit the unfulfilling relationship to look for someone more suited for her. Another bonus: her debilitating headaches stopped.

When we have more than one internal voice speaking to us, how do we know which thoughts to heed? Go with the gentle one, the voice whose message makes you feel understood and appreciated. The more you identify with the loving voice, the more readily you will be able to recognize it when it arises. The negative voice gives credence to the most horrible things you believe about yourself. Your critical voice is a belief system you bought into at some point in your life that doesn't work for you. It never did, and you can stop it now.

Stop It!

There is a funny skit from *MADtv* in which Bob Newhart plays a psychiatrist. A woman comes into his office and complains of being plagued by negative thoughts. The psychiatrist explains his billing schedule: $5 for the first 5 minutes, and he assures her the treatment won't take longer than that. Then he leans forward very seriously and says her problem can be solved in two words. Then he shouts, "STOP IT!" [21]

She is of course deeply upset by this advice. Bob then asks her if she wants to spend her entire life being plagued by irrational thoughts and negative thinking. Of course, she doesn't. "So, stop it!" he exclaims.

It's funny because yes, of course, that is the answer. It's so simple, and yet it's so profoundly difficult. Most of us think that our problems will never go away. While not all of us are frequent visitors to the therapist's couch, we all have thoughts that occasionally plague us—be they irrational fears, difficult chapters in our pasts or a current challenge.

Studies correlate our outlook and emotional wellbeing with heart health, diabetes, hypertension, and even the common cold. [22] But I don't need to convince you that you want to be happier, that's an easy sell. What everyone wants to know is how to be happier—how to let go of all those thoughts that keep us from being happy. That's the key. Worrying about a situation in no way makes it better.

It's not the situation that causes unhappiness—it's our thoughts and feelings surrounding it.

I love this adage: I don't worry, because it's inefficient! How do we stop thinking these destructive, unhappy thoughts? You have to yell, "STOP IT." And you have to mean it. Some days in my counseling of couples, all I want to do is shout "stop it," but this isn't something we can do for someone else. So let's take a closer look at the dynamics of unhappiness and how we can put an end to it.

As Within, So Without

Very often, we create unhappiness. It doesn't matter where it stems from; it matters where it rests and how it consumes you and those around you. Your job may feel tedious. You may have agreed to do something, and now you resent it. You may be harboring ill will for someone close to you. This negative energy is harmful, not just to you, but to lots of other people around you.

It doesn't make a difference whether or not your thoughts or emotions about the situation are justified.

What you feel internally is what you create externally. Therefore, you create unhappiness, stress, peace, and joy, internally and externally, regardless of who or what you perceive is the cause for it. You are responsible for how everything affects you, and thereby how you affect others.

So how do we drop negative feelings? Bob Newhart put us on the right track. How do you drop a piece of burning coal that you're holding in your hand or a piece of useless baggage you're carrying? When you recognize that you're no longer willing to suffer the pain any longer, you let it go.

"As within, so without" is a principle that speaks to every area of our lives, but even more so to our relationship.

As your inner life begins to change, your outer life will follow suit.

So how do we dispel negative thoughts from our minds?

Step 1. Focus your attention on what's important. The kabbalists teach that this world is called Olam Hafuch, which means "an upside-down world." The things that are important to us often turn out to be unimportant and things that seem unimportant turn out to be the most important. In short, we focus on the wrong things.

Step 2. Don't try to quell your thoughts. It usually takes a hundred or more pre-thoughts to create one dominant thought. The irony here is likely apparent to anyone who has ever been on a diet. When you restrict your diet, all you think about is the food that you are not allowing yourself to eat.

As Eckhart Tolle says, "Whatever you fight, you strengthen, and what you resist, persists." [23] Instead of trying to repel negative thoughts, acknowledge them. Consider whether they support you or hold you back. Paying momentary attention to a thought doesn't mean you accept it as truth, but it does provide you the opportunity to firmly dismiss it as inaccurate.

Step 3: Think about positive things. Consider the people you love, the things that inspire you, and everything you are grateful for. You can't combat negativity by ignoring it, just as you can't make a dark room light by pretending it isn't dark! But you can create Light in your mind by focusing on, and affirming the thoughts that bring you joy, confidence, and peace.

Step 4: Identify one frequent thought you have that is utter nonsense. Common examples include *I can't do it; I'm not good enough; I never get what I want*. Perhaps you've deemed a situation hopeless or written off a relationship. Check your consciousness and become open to seeing where it may have led you astray.

Step 5: Be aware of who you choose to surround yourself with. Environment is important. You are the company you keep. Analyze what energy you are allowing to affect and influence you and be conscious of what kind of energy you are expressing to the world. Your thoughts create your reality – this is the irrefutable power of the mind.

"No problem can be solved from the same level of consciousness that created it." — Albert Einstein [24]

Thoughts are the currency of daily existence, and they have the power to gather and increase in magnitude.

Louise Hay said, "Imagine your thoughts are like drops of water. When you think the same thoughts over and over again you create this incredible body of water, at first a puddle, then a pond, then a lake, and finally an ocean. If our thoughts are negative, we drown in a sea of negativity. If our thoughts are positive, we float in the ocean of life." [25] What Louise is saying so poetically is that your thoughts become your beliefs and your beliefs inform the choices you make. This is not meant to overwhelm you, a thought is just a thought, and a thought can be changed. It instead is intended to inspire you and to awaken you to the power of thought.

Chapter Seven

Understanding Emotions as Signals

KABBALISTIC PRINCIPLE:

**Our emotions are tremendously powerful
and can either assist us or limit us.**

. . . .

Our emotions are fluid—they arise suddenly and can shift easily. Although we can predict how we might feel about a given circumstance, at the moment, our emotions are largely involuntary. For example, a man walks into a doctor's office. It's a beautiful day outside, everything is going well, and he's happy. Then the doctor comes in and says, "I have bad news. Your test results are back, and you have a serious illness." What happens? The patient becomes understandably distraught. His mind may go blank. He may need to take the rest of the day off work to think about his situation, figure out whom to call, and begin to put his affairs in order.

Then, a few hours later, the doctor calls and says, "Oops, I'm terribly sorry, I misread your test results. You're fine." Now the patient is understandably elated. But during this emotional rollercoaster, nothing actually changed. The patient's health was the same from beginning to end, yet his emotional life went on a white-knuckle ride.

Psychologists have identified a phenomenon known as an "affect heuristic." [26] Very simply, this is a mental shortcut we take that allows us to make quick decisions based on past experience. Subconsciously our brains are constantly making "like" or "don't like" judgments that affect our

67

choices. Drawing on them is the equivalent of "going with your gut." For instance, if I use the phrase "island vacation," it likely evokes a feeling of relaxation, whereas if I say "heart disease," it will probably elicit concern. However, everyone has a different set of affect heuristics based on their life experience. As social psychologist Robert Zajonk put it, "Feelings are not free of thought, and thoughts are not free of feelings." [27]

Neurologists have discovered that people who sustain brain damage in specific areas of the brain experience a loss of emotion. [28] Social psychologist Jonathan Haidt writes about this phenomenon in his book *The Happiness Hypothesis*. [29] Patients with this type of brain damage report not feeling emotion when they should, yet their logic and reason remain unaffected, along with their understanding of social mores. Since we often struggle with our emotions, you might think that not having any might make life easier. Like Mr. Spock in *Star Trek,* these patients could now rely exclusively on the rational mind to make good choices. But this proved not to be the case. In fact, it was quite the opposite.

People who were unable to conjure up any feelings saw their lives fall apart. Rather than turning into purely goal-oriented, hyper-focused people, they found themselves unable to make even the simplest decision. Without the help of the affect heuristic, these patients were paralyzed. In the absence of feeling we have no desire, and in the absence of desire, we don't know which way to go. As Dr. Haidt put it, "Human rationality depends on sophisticated emotionality. It is only that our emotional brains work so well that our reasoning brains can work at all." [30] Simply put, emotions provide us with a feedback system. They inform our worldview and influence our thoughts.

One way to become more skillful with your emotions is to take the time to get in touch with them throughout the day. You can go from elation to frustration in a moment, and checking in with your feelings can help you understand why they fluctuate, seemingly without warning.

A Closer Look at Emotional Feedback

Most people treat their emotions as truth, rather than data. I want you to rethink this. Our emotions don't dictate who we are—they are only signals of what's going on inside. The great power of our emotions is that we can use them as indicators of what's going on in our minds and our souls. Emotions clue us in to how we feel about people and situations. Some of us look forward to feedback, and some of us prefer to avoid it. When the feedback we're getting feels good, we welcome it, but if it triggers anxiety, fear, or anger, we may try to disconnect from it through avoidance, or self-medication. Feelings are difficult for everyone. I know a woman who is always *doing* something, every waking minute. She is constantly avoiding her thoughts because they are usually negative and aimed inward. She's especially uncomfortable with silence because in silence, her thoughts blare. The father of a friend of mine also couldn't tolerate his feelings because they spoke to his loneliness. He was so uncomfortable being alone that he kept a TV on in every room.

Our emotions inform us, they guide us, and they show us when it's time for change. They serve as a signal that something we're doing or thinking isn't to our benefit, or they affirm that the path we're on is the right one. Many people fear that once they open the floodgates of emotion, they'll be swallowed up. I assure you this isn't the case. You can choose to simply observe your feelings without getting swept up in them. Assume a higher-level perspective, that of a scientist. Simply watch, like watching a scary movie. You may experience excitement, fear, or nervousness. You're not in the film, but you can still experience the thrill of it while remaining an observer. You're aware of what you're feeling, but you're choosing a different response.

Emotions are nuanced and complex. Often we may be experiencing an emotion that stems from an even deeper feeling. Jealousy, for example, can be an attention-seeking behavior, or it can arise from a lack of self-esteem, or it can result from a fear of being replaced. So, which one is it? This is where observation comes in.

I work out with a woman who is a self-described "jealous person." After being single for a while, she entered into a relationship. She was often enraged with her boyfriend because she was convinced he was going to leave her, although he wasn't flirting with other women and showed no desire to end the relationship. The only thing that could drive them apart, he told her, was her jealousy. So I gave her an exercise.

The first step was to bring awareness to the emotion. Every time she felt jealous, I asked her to observe the emotion instead of reacting to it to get to the root of the cause. Eventually, she realized that her jealousy developed because she believed she wasn't good enough for him. Now that she figured that out, she realized she could direct her focus toward herself and away from her boyfriend. When painful emotions arise, like anger and jealousy, we have the option to keep them to ourselves or to communicate what we're feeling. With our partners, the latter approach can be very effective.

Reacting looks like this. *"I know you're flirting with other women, so you might as well just leave me now. Get out!"* Communicating looks like: *"At this moment, I am feeling jealousy because when you say/do/behave in this way, it makes me feel insecure."* Communicating through emotion supports connection, reacting drives disconnection.

I asked my friend to make a list of the things she does that make her feel good about herself. Then I asked her to identify what emotions lie behind those things. She came up with words like empowered, creative, and strong. Behind her good feelings lie qualities that are a fundamental part of who she is. Those qualities are not going to change, although sometimes she may lose sight of them. I asked her to think about this list whenever her self-esteem felt a little shaky.

Observing our emotions closely is imperative if we're going to understand how they affect our lives and those of the people we love.

Acknowledge Your Default Emotion

We all have a default emotion that takes center stage when we're feeling stressed. Mine is sadness. What's yours? Among the most common are anger, fear, resentment, or shame.

My first experience with sadness happened after my family had moved from Louisiana to California, following a devastating financial setback. I identified my default emotion years later when I found myself in a place of deep sadness once again after struggling with an eating disorder. Generally, I'm upbeat, yet when met with extreme opposition, I experience sadness. When this occurs, I know something is going on that I need to pay attention to.

If you aren't sure what your default emotion is, think back to how you felt during two or three instances when things didn't go your way. You were let go from a job, went through a breakup, lost an opportunity you'd been counting on...whatever it may have been. Under pressure, we all have a default emotion, and it's probably one you're pretty familiar with.

Kristen's default emotion is anger. Kristen is typically sweet, kind, and good-hearted. However, when something challenges her, she meets it with anger. Her oldest daughter knows how to push all of her buttons. Kristen will mention what a beautiful day it is. In response, her daughter will complain that it's too windy, she's cold, and she wants to go home. Kristen becomes outrageously angry when her daughter expresses dissatisfaction about anything. It was getting to the point where she was beginning to feel that her rage was defining who she was. She began thinking of herself as an angry person. She asked me about anger management courses. I replied that consistent anger is probably a symptom, so let's identify its root cause. It takes a lot of energy to fight what you're feeling.

Identify the emotion (data) and choose a response.

Kristen's task was not to create a change in her daughter, but to work through why her daughter's actions and perspectives were so irritating to her. Kristen revealed she had a complicated relationship with her mother, and they sometimes wouldn't talk to each other for years. Therefore, it was a priority for Kristen to have a close relationship with her daughter. Whenever her daughter complained or disagreed (as children tend to do), rather than use that as the basis for a conversation, Kristen felt that her most valuable relationship was under attack. So she responded with anger. Her daughter's behavior affected her so much because she desired to have a 'perfect' mother-daughter relationship. Once she connected her reaction with the underlying cause, she was able to control her anger.

Choose what to pay attention to and how to derive meaning from your emotions, because they arise for a reason. You can't pretend emotions away. Rising above your emotional upheaval can transform your relationship.

Chapter Eight

Radical Accountability

Becoming the best version of ourselves means taking responsibility for the areas where we need to grow. However, these areas are often dark and extremely sensitive. They keep us trapped in victim mentalities. Although victimhood manifests in a variety of ways, such as denial, anxiety, and resentment, it is born of three negative emotions. I call them the Big Three: guilt, blame, and shame, and they are almost always the driving force behind every part of our lives that we wish would change.

Let's distinguish between guilt, blame, and shame—feelings that most of us often cycle through. Understanding what you're feeling gives you a better chance of not taking it on. For example, if another driver damages your car, then you may feel angry. But if a hailstorm caused the damage, you might feel sad. In both of these cases, whether you are angry or sad, you are still *blaming* an outside source for your car's damage. If you were personally responsible, let's say you were texting while driving, then you'd most likely feel *guilt* or *shame*.

- Guilt: *I did something bad, and I am afraid of how I will be judged for it, both by myself and by others.*
- Blame: *You are responsible for how I feel.*
- Shame: *I AM bad. Not only did I do something bad, but I am also a bad person, and when you find out the truth, you'll reject me.*

Then there's anger. Though it isn't one of the Big Three, it goes hand-in-hand with them and can be just as destructive. Anger is often a reaction to what has happened to a person. The angrier the person is, the more they are blaming something or someone else. If there is a circumstance that upsets you and you feel anger around it, remember that anger is just a response to a perceived injustice.

Many people mistake anger for strength when, in fact, anger is just the hallmark reaction of a victim.

It has the same catalyst as sadness, but anger is external while sadness is internal.

Guilt

One of my favorite words is unassailable. When you're unassailable, you can't be attacked or defeated. This word resonates with me because during various times in my life, I have been on the receiving end of blame and judgment, and my first reaction used to be guilt. In my Middle Eastern family, guilt was a commonplace emotion. In my adult life, guilt led to shame. My solution was to try to create perfection in every aspect of my life because if something is perfect, it is unassailable. There is no way to criticize perfection, because, well…it's perfect. I dedicated myself to building protective walls against vulnerability by pursuing perfection.

Much later on, when I finally saw this strategy wasn't creating the desired result, I shifted gears and moved in a more productive direction. Now it wasn't physical, or even emotional, perfection I was seeking. It was an unassailable consciousness—meaning getting to a place where I could maintain my consciousness, even in times where I felt judged and under attack. I could use the opportunity to develop my character. As a result, my core self wasn't shaken by harsh words, criticism, or reactions.

At times when I did feel blame and judgment, I chose to let them go, like water off a duck's back. I decided that if I felt I had done something wrong, I would make an effort to do it differently next time. It's been quite a journey, and I'm still on the road. The realization that guilt and shame were not inevitable—and that perfection wasn't the only way to avoid them—has been extraordinarily freeing for me.

When things happen to any of us in life—be it an abusive childhood, a failed marriage, or the inability to conceive a child—adopting an unassailable consciousness can help you from identifying with your circumstances. However, difficult as those situations are, they don't define who I am.

Blame

Not too long ago I had to go to the dentist, and for the record, I hate going to the dentist. After she poked and prodded for what felt like forever, she said, "You need a crown. Your fillings are starting to break down, and there's some trouble with your gums." She continued on and on, you get the point. I realized at that moment that what I don't like about the dentist isn't just the Novocain; it's feeling like a failure. As though I have not adequately taken care of my teeth throughout my entire life, and I can't do anything about it at this point. There I am, sitting in the dentist's chair, feeling the unwanted feelings of being a failure when a thought cropped up.

"This is my husband's fault."

Yep. I wanted someone to blame, and he was candidate number one. Have you ever found that it is somehow easiest to blame those closest to you? In moments when we are feeling negative emotions, we tend to blame our partners. And usually, we blame them for things we would never blame on anyone else: disappointments, unhappiness, unworthiness, and failures. All the things for which we are inherently responsible. By blaming my husband for my disappointing dental report, I didn't have to take responsibility for the state of my teeth. I was casting myself in the role of the victim.

We all fall into this trap, myself included. There I sat, truly ruminating, as ridiculous as it sounds, over the fact that if Michael had better dental hygiene, I would too. The thought I caught was, *"I haven't taken care of my teeth because he's rubbed off on me!"* I brought awareness to this thought and, of course, started to laugh, because it's ludicrous. But honestly, it was my initial thought in the face of feeling like a dental hygiene failure.

Accountability and blame are not the same. Accountability holds someone responsible for their actions. Blame holds someone responsible for how we feel. It's justified to hold an ex-spouse to their commitment to pay child support. It's not justified to make your ex responsible for your continued emotional suffering and inability to enter into a new relationship.

Instead of saying, "why me?" when something happens, ask:
"Why has this situation come into my life?"
"What can I learn from this situation? How can I grow?"

By posing these questions, we stop casting blame on ourselves, someone else, or something external. If you are placing blame, you don't see options or opportunities because you're focusing on the perceived unfairness of the situation instead of focusing on a solution.

Shame

Shame means we think there is something so awful about us that if other people discovered it, we would no longer be worthy of a connection to hem. This is a painful way to live.

Many people who struggle with issues of self-worth and self-loathing had parents who used shame as a parenting tool. This teaches children that they are not inherently worthy of love.

The way we talk to our children becomes the inner voice in their head, their inner critic. If you relate to either the parent or the child, more than likely, you are creating those situations throughout your life because shame is familiar to you. It's what you know.

It is possible to overcome shame. Dr. Brené Brown says that to do so, there are three things we need to know:
- Shame is universal. We all experience it. The only people without shame are people who have antisocial personality disorders (psychopaths or sociopaths).
- We're afraid to talk about it because shame feels ugly. Our shameful secrets grow stronger in the dark, but by not keeping them a secret, they can't grow.

- The more we talk about shame, the less control it has over our lives. The minute our shame is shared and exposed to the light, maybe after a momentary shock of horror and recognition, poof! They're gone.[31]

Shame lurks in the most common areas of our lives, like body image, parenting, addiction, sex, and aging. To feel shame is to be human. Yet, shame is a belief we have about ourselves, and beliefs are choices and can be changed.

Nobody has to earn worthiness. Our worth is inherent. Any shame we feel is disrespectful to ourselves, and it spills over into every area of life.

You may be choosing to overfeed your body, or self-medicate with excessive alcohol, or pills. You may convey your lack of self-respect in the way you carry yourself, how you dress, or even how you treat others. Things are not as isolated as we wish to believe.

When you do meet someone special, that critical voice in your head may think, "You must have low standards if you love me."

Releasing the Big Three

Many people live with shame their entire lives because something terrible happened to them, or they made a mistake and have decided they are inherently undeserving. Many people place blame anywhere and everywhere else to avoid facing their shame. And so the cycle of victimhood continues—until you decide to break it.

To change negative emotional patterns of blame, guilt, and shame, practice the following exercise:

- Recognize that the feelings you are holding onto don't serve you. When you feel blame, guilt, or shame, think back to an event, as early as you can remember, when you felt that way. Don't relive the event, simply try watching as an observer and see the situation for what it actually was, rather than how it felt.

- Identify the coping mechanism you have used in the past to deal with difficult situations. Was it placing blame? Was it guilt? Was it shame?

- Now, remind yourself that you can choose to see any experience in a completely new light. Take full responsibility for your happiness and well-being in the present.

KABBALISTIC PRINCIPLE:

**Each one of us is personally responsible
for our success or failure in life.**

· · · · · · · ·

Self-Handicapping and Other Forms of Self-Sabotage

Self-handicapping is a scientific phrase coined by Berglas and Jones, explaining what we do to ourselves when we lack confidence. It protects our self-image wherein we choose failure over damaging our self-image. [32] For example, a student may decide not to study to keep from feeling bad about themselves if they get poor grades. After all, they didn't study, so that explains the low score. Some people, when faced with a relationship issue they don't know how to navigate, knowingly or not, protect their sense of self-confidence by externalizing the blame onto outside circumstances that they in fact set up themselves. It's self-deception at its worst. It allows you to cast blame on your partner instead of working on yourself. It's the relationship version of a designated issue.

If someone knows that a difficult conversation awaits them at home, they may absentmindedly goof off all day, so they are forced to work late. Or a partner may come to the couple's counseling session with a hangover.

Partying the night before a test, skipping practice before a big game, purposefully reconnecting with an ex right before your wedding: by creating these less-than-optimum scenarios, you don't feel so bad about failure.

Let's look at a wife whose husband is difficult to please. He often finds flaws in her personality, and she feels like she's constantly disappointing him, mostly because he tells her so. Because she anticipates his disappointment, she may burn dinner "accidentally" to avoid hearing his usual criticism of the meal. If dinner is ruined, then they'll go out, or order in, and whatever they end up eating for dinner isn't going to be her fault. When people have a good excuse, they are less motivated to improve themselves. It is self-paralysis which ensures that things stay exactly as they are. Of course, this isn't what we want, so why do we continue? Because even unhealthy behavior has a payoff.

One way to change self-sabotaging behavior is to find the reason you are choosing to engage in it. Berglas and Jones argued that some people turn to substances like alcohol to avoid the implications of negative feedback for failure and to enhance positive feedback for success. [33] If you self-handicap with strategies known to undermine performance and you fail, now you can externalize the blame — and protect your sense of competence. You didn't score poorly on the exam because you are not intelligent, or don't know the material. You scored low because you were hungover, high, exhausted, or dehydrated. When you have something external to blame, you don't need to blame yourself. Failure is now less embarrassing because you can rationalize it as not being your fault.

The problem with that strategy is that while failure hurts and can be embarrassing or even humiliating, it's also a pilot light for motivation. Think about it. Bring to mind one experience where you felt embarrassed or humiliated, and you'll probably find you used that feeling to push yourself to do better next time.

From Sabotage to Sight

Growing up, there was a sticker on the refrigerator that said, "Life is short; eat dessert first." I loved that saying, which is ironic, because at that time

I didn't eat dessert at all, much less first. There was nothing in my life that even felt or tasted sweet. For a time, food for me was nothing more than an aspect I could control in my life; to be able to dictate when I should eat versus reacting to my body's desires. I gained strength in not desiring it at all. At the time, I believed that I deserved the very minimum in life, including food, although at the time, I didn't see the correlation. I felt so emotionally empty inside that I made myself physically empty.

The result was a 5-year battle with anorexia and body dysmorphia. My perception of myself was distorted. It was the darkest and saddest time of my life. I felt so alone, so lost, and without a clue as to who I was. These feelings were so uncomfortable for me that I wanted to jump out of my skin.

I never believed that anyone was meant to live a life of unhappiness, and yet for some reason, I did not hold that same belief for myself. I didn't feel that I deserved love or happiness. Therefore, I didn't give myself permission or the voice to express any desires for myself.

Throughout the experience, I asked myself, "What is propelling me to starve myself nearly to death? Why would I do this to myself? What is so unfulfilling in my life that I would physically sabotage myself in this way?" Because I never found answers, I would run—literally. I was always running something off: frustration, fear, a desire for freedom. I wanted to run until I was so tired and depleted that no one could take anything from me because there was nothing left to give. I usually only felt a comforting nothingness after a 20-mile run. I did this a few times a week, at which point I was left too tired to fight, to want, to desire or dream.

Along with running, there was another practice I adhered to. Every day I would go into the bathroom, and conduct a pinch-test—grabbing bits of skin between my thumb and index finger to ensure I had no fat deposits. It was a thorough investigation I performed every day. If I'm being honest, I did this anytime I passed a mirror. Yet, I still couldn't see the harm I was doing. Until one morning...I was in the bathroom, my nightshirt pulled up above my waist, conducting yet another pinch-test in front of the mirror when I caught sight of myself. Suddenly, I broke free of my trance. Instead of seeing the obese person I usually saw, I saw what I really looked like. I was a skeletal, virtually unrecognizable stranger. I was horrified. I mean, *truly* horrified. I saw no resemblance to the girl that had stared back at me for the first 19 years of my life. In the mirror was a young woman who was well on the way to slowly killing herself. I started to panic, screaming for my mother at the top of my lungs. Crying, we hugged each other as if we were both hanging on for dear life.

I had finally *seen* myself, taken in the effects of my self-sabotage. I recognized the damage I had done. Later, when I reached a more in-depth understanding through my studies in Kabbalah, I came to call this moment the gift of sight. At that moment, I understood, inescapably, that I had a problem. I needed to fix it, and I had to believe that no matter what false sense of reality I would see after that moment, it was not true, no matter how real it felt.

There is a portion in the Bible called Re'eh, which means "to see." Re'eh is about the ability to see blessings and curses that manifest according to the energy with which we act. When we understand something, we say, "I see." This refers to our cognitive understanding of a concept, not the actualization of a physical manifestation.

In that moment of Re'eh I saw it all. I was lonely, and I wanted to be loved. Through Kabbalah, I came to realize that to be loved I would have to give love, and in order to give love, I would have to find the source of that love inside myself. I'd been sabotaging myself because I believed I was unlovable. I could see where my choices were going to take me, and I made a conscious decision to change the outcome.

We all have areas in our life we know we are running away from. Once they are called into the light, once they are seen, they no longer have the same power to derail our lives. You realize that it was never you running from it, it was running you.

Moving from self-sabotage to awareness is how we become radically accountable.

It means gazing unflinchingly at the most troubled and difficult parts of yourself. You can't be authentic if you're hiding parts of who you are, and only you can be the one to acknowledge them. Let these neglected areas be *seen* so that true transformation can begin.

Love the Opposition

When we finally succeed in taking steps toward healing and transformation, we may find that not everyone is supportive. When you begin to make changes, you're going to run into some immediate, sometimes powerful opposition. This is a good thing! The best indication that we're on the right path is opposition from the people around us. Spiritual work *requires* opposition. If you are going to do something big in the world, there has to be a force opposing you.

I began studying Kabbalah at the age of 17 and became committed to my studies by 18. When my family noticed how devoted I had become to my spiritual work, I began receiving some not-so-positive feedback from one of my uncles. And when he started criticizing, the rest of the family would join in. The irony here is that my family had encouraged me to study Kabbalah in the first place! Still, the more involved I got, the more opposition I received.

Week after week, I was interrogated. "What are you doing? What are you learning? What are you studying? Does that really work?" And my every answer led to more judgment. "You're too extreme. You don't know what you're doing with your life. You're too young. You're being brainwashed."

This barrage brought me to a new level of awareness. At first, I did a lot of checking in with myself. "Do I believe in this? Is this truly my path?" The answer was always yes. Once I was certain, something shifted inside me. The opposition forced me to challenge myself. It served to clarify my beliefs and hardened my resolve to live by them. I recognized that it was necessary on some level. I could see how that the slightest bit of doubt, even 1%, had created an opening for negativity. It gave my uncle room to challenge me. I tried everything to make him leave me alone. I tried to ignore him. That didn't work. I tried to argue. That didn't work. Only when I made the decision that I was 100% sure that the wisdom of Kabbalah was my calling, did my uncle never utter another word because there were no ears to hear it. I closed the opening with my certainty.

This concept of opposition played out in the real-life story of race car champions James Hunt and Niki Lauda, whose famous rivalry was dramatized in Ron Howard's 2013 film *Rush*. A horrific accident during one of their races left Niki Lauda severely burned over much of his body. During those torturous months in the hospital, he would watch James Hunt's races on television, all the while screaming at the TV about how much he hated him. One day while getting his lungs pumped and vacuumed, his doctor said to him, "Stop thinking of it as a curse that you have been given an enemy in life. It can be a blessing, too. A wise man gets more from his enemies than a fool does from his friends."

Niki Lauda realized that without his arch-enemy, he never would have been so motivated to make a full recovery—which he did. Without James challenging him, he probably never would have become the great driver he was. Eventually, the two men met and talked about what happened. When James said, "In many ways, I feel responsible for what happened..." Niki cut him off. "You were. But trust me, watching you win those races while I was fighting for my life made you equally responsible for getting me back in the car." [34]

The transformation that allowed them to become friends occurred the moment they stopped seeing their difficulties with one another as being personal. Instead of making it about that 'awful' person and feeling hatred towards each other, they realized that their 'enemy' was actually their blessing, pushing them toward greatness. Once they understood this, they were able to transform their vengeance into an appreciation for the opposition. It's only human to resist opposition. If you feel opposition in your relationship—or any other aspect of your life—see it for what it is. It's a gift pointing you in the direction of your highest self.

Opposition from our partner helps us more than we know. We all need someone supporting, challenging, and reminding us of the characteristics that *don't* serve us. The only way we can see our reflection in a mirror is if we stand "opposed" to it. If you can't see yourself, how can you know where you need to improve?

This gift can also be a couple's greatest challenge. Not everyone *wants* a mirror. Not everyone wants to let go of victimhood. Not everyone wants to change. And we cannot inspire that want or that choice in anyone. Because helping people is part of my life's work, I take great satisfaction in assisting couples to get through hard times. Usually, I'm able to help a marriage get back on track. But sometimes I'm not. It all depends on the couple, their dedication to the work, and their level of commitment to each other and themselves. As Kabbalist Rav Ashlag said, "You can never do the work for somebody else."

Chapter Nine

You Are Lovable

Kabbalist Rav Ashlag shared a parable about a wealthy man who had prepared a new room for his son by filling it with gold, silver, fine clothing, a remarkable library, and everything else that his son could want or need. However, upon finally entering the room, it was so dark that his son was unable to see anything. After such high expectations, he wept with disappointment. There he sat, heavy-hearted. All he needed to do to dispel his gloom was to pull open the heavy curtains. If he let in the sunlight, he could see the storehouse of treasures that had been laid out for him.

We're all a bit like the son sitting in the dark. We tend to see only what we lack. When in reality, everything we need is already here.

KABBALISTIC PRINCIPLE:

Blessings are waiting to come to us, but cannot
rest in a place of darkness — where we feel lack,
sadness or undeserving.

. . . .

Feeling undeserving is like saying to the Creator, "I've given up," or "I'm hopeless." The Talmud tells us that if a person loses something, but does not give up hope of finding it, he will eventually recover it. However, if he loses hope of recovering it, whoever finds it will become its rightful owner. There is danger in feeling lack because that invites more lack to come to us. Our thoughts become self-fulfilling prophecies. We sabotage ourselves because we cannot draw blessings and love into our lives while we're thinking badly of ourselves—they are opposing realities. It's entirely up to you how many blessings you are able to draw into your life. To bring about miraculous changes, begin by taking small actions; these create openings for the Creator to work through.

We All Deserve Love

A highly successful wedding planner, Susan had been raped when she was six years old, and the abuse had continued into her teens. She kept this secret and the shame she felt to herself until she divulged it to me. For decades Susan had felt responsible for the childhood abuse, certain that she must be a deeply damaged person to have attracted those terrible assaults. Susan desperately wanted to be in a relationship, but try as she might, she was unsuccessful in finding one. Susan had the belief that she didn't deserve happiness. She was 47, but she was stuck at six, blaming herself for the actions of her abuser.

I told her that there was nothing she did that caused her to be raped and that her essence is pure and perfect. The undeniable reality is that to some degree, most of us allow our thoughts around feeling undeserving or unloved to permeate into our lives and overtake them. We all deserve to be fulfilled and happy. Truly loving yourself is an unconditional process that allows you to accept, celebrate, and appreciate all you are, both positive and negative, completely and authentically. It also gives you permission to alter the things about yourself that don't serve you.

Life is filled with experiences and people who serve to mirror aspects of ourselves; everyone we meet has something to teach us. We often place importance on the wrong things, on the bad things that happen to us, rather than the things that are truly of value. There is one relationship in particular that we tend to neglect —the one we have with the Creator—yet it's the one relationship that has always been constant, even if we have no memory of it in this lifetime. It's where we come from, and where we return.

Tell Your Secret

How could Susan expect to fall in love when she wasn't coming from a place of loving herself? When we hate who we are, especially because of something traumatic that has happened to us, it's difficult to change how we feel about ourselves. Sharing these negative thoughts and feelings is the quickest way to release them. Don't keep them a secret. People come to my office all the time and share regret for past actions and shame for the things they have done. The second they see *my* reaction, which is always supportive, they can give themselves permission to see another perspective, and begin the process of forgiving themselves.

Moments when we accuse ourselves of being 'incompetent,' 'lazy,' 'irresponsible,' or 'selfish' are the moments when that negative voice inside us, which some psychotherapists call the "inner critic," has taken over. Instead of berating yourself this way, try speaking to yourself as you would to a child. You would never tell a small child she was stupid, so what makes you think it's okay to speak to yourself this way? If you can quiet the inner critic, you will hear a softer, gentler voice that lies deeper within you. This is your authentic inner voice, the one that is kind and forgiving. This soft voice speaks for the core of our being, where we are all perfect.

Attracting Authentic Love

Loving yourself means loving all of yourself, even the things that are hard to look at. This is unconditional love.

If you can't offer yourself unconditional love, you won't be able to offer it to anyone else, either.

Nor will you be able to receive it. You can begin to cultivate unconditional love—for yourself and others—in the following two ways:

1. **Express appreciation** Sometimes at the end of a very long day, I will turn to my husband and tell him how grateful I am for all that he is, for all that he gives me, and for making this life journey so worthwhile. And while I'm practicing gratitude, I give myself a little pat on the back for so wisely choosing such a great life partner. It works both ways; appreciating our loved ones confirms our appreciation for ourselves.

2. **Focus on the good** As we've seen, one of the biggest deterrents in achieving our goals is negative thinking. We may not want to admit it, but we've all had thoughts like Susan's—that we're not deserving, that we are damaged because of our past and therefore we don't deserve good things. It's amazing how skillful we can be at criticizing ourselves. But by bringing awareness to the blessings in our lives, we can shift our focus.

To attract authentic love, we must know that we are perfect and deserving. Often we find ourselves looking at a friend or an acquaintance and think, "Oh, they're so lucky, they have it all; life is so easy for them." Not true. No one is more, nor less, deserving than you. The Creator's intent for every one of us is a life of happiness and fulfillment. You don't have to earn love any more than you do the right to breathe. Don't allow anyone's negative opinions or prejudices to make you think you're not good enough. You are deserving of love. It's as simple as that. Accept this and know this.

Part Two

Moving from Me to We

Happily Ever After (For Real)

Chapter Ten

The Cinderella Syndrome

Love is one of the most widely covered topics in the world, and yet, surprisingly, it's also one of the most misunderstood. That's because we see so many distorted images of love in song and verse, in novels and on-screen romance. After all the dramatic obstacles have been overcome, the camera zooms out, the violins come up, and the couple walks off together into an idyllic sunset. But what happens after the credits roll?

What we see in the movies is what I'll identify as romantic love—a passionate attachment between two people, a dizzy the-room-is-spinning kind of feeling that fills the stomach with excitement and butterflies. We hear that falling in love is about "following our heart, not our mind," and that love itself is magical and beyond reason. But if it is really love that we feel, we feel it for a reason; that reason may not be conscious or logical, but it does exist. However, love that is solely based on feelings is a form of love that cannot last. Just as positive emotions are insufficient for lasting happiness, so, too, are strong feelings insufficient to sustain love.

Consider this: we put ourselves through every imaginable uncomfortable situation to meet The One: online dating, double dating, blind dating (oh, the horror). Eventually, through great effort, we do meet The One, and we've been led to believe that we will live "happily ever after." The problem is that most movies are about where love begins. It's the "living-happily-ever-after" part that poses the greatest challenge. It's after "the sunset" when difficulties often arise.

"The finest love stories come after the marriage, not before." [35]
— Irving Stone

When it comes to relationships and marriage, most of us hold cherished illusions that true love will resolve all of our problems and take away all our insecurities. We believe the right person could even provide enough love for both of us. We need to dispel this notion that our relationships can transport us anywhere, whether it's a white-picket fence in the suburbs or a house in Beverly Hills. The idea of romance and marriage as a ticket to bliss is a total fallacy.

I've counseled numerous couples over the years—some who have been married as little as a month, some a year, and others for decades—all of whom find themselves considering why they signed up for marriage in the first place, or why they have stayed married as long as they have. "What was I thinking?" is a common refrain. Even though marriage can be difficult, this question still surprises me. I respond with questions of my own. "What did you think it would be? What did you expect? What did you look for going into the relationship? How did you feel about your partner? What do you think happened to those feelings?"

Americans place a high value on marriage. It holds a central place in our dreams. But 40-50% of marriages in the United States end in divorce. [36] Perhaps this is because we have a consumer mindset that can seep into our romantic lives. We end up believing that there's a transactional aspect of marriage, where we're constantly looking for what we're getting from the relationship. It's the customer versus the provider mentality. We have the perception that marriage is all about me, for meeting MY needs, not about what I do, but about how it makes me feel. I deserve better than I'm getting. Can anyone say sense of entitlement?

Often we assign others to be something in our life that they never asked to be, and probably don't want to be. It wasn't a responsibility that we should have given them in the first place. An unrealistic expectation looks something like this common scenario:

A wife has been home all day with the kids, and just as her patience is wearing thin, she has a run-in with her teenage son. She feels as if she didn't handle the situation well, and she wants her husband's reassurance and support the second he walks in the door. She unrealistically expects him to be 100% available to her from that moment on. After all, she's done the heavy lifting all day with the children, and now it's his turn. She isn't looking for support from her husband in that moment. She's looking for a superhero to come to the rescue.

A better approach would be to consider that maybe her husband had his own rough day. He needs her support as well, and is desperate for a few moments to unwind and decompress. An alternative approach to get his help would be to call him on his way home and give him the heads up about the situation and her needs. This is how we begin to manage our unrealistic expectations. No one can be all the things we expect them to be. If you don't appoint, you won't be disappointed.

We have the tendency in our culture to treat friendships and life partners as a commodity, or an investment. We put something in with the expectation that we'll get something out. When we don't get what we expected, the disappointment we feel inevitably feels very personal, so we blame our partners for our unhappiness. In many relationships, there's a dynamic where one wants more from the other.

We fall victim to the illusion that if this person is "the one" for me, our relationship is going to be problem-free. This is not realistic. No relationship is without tension. In the end, the problems we often have in relationships are less because we're with the wrong person, and more because of our issues we've failed to resolve.

Every relationship goes through difficulties. Just look at Romeo and Juliet. Or go back even further to biblical times. Abraham and Sara had trouble conceiving. Rebecca and Isaac had a very negative child. Jacob wanted to marry Rachel, but ended up marrying her sister Leah and had to wait seven years to marry Rachel. (If you're a man reading this, two wives may not sound like such a bad thing.)

Illusions burden love with unrealistic expectations. Women in particular fall victim to the "Cinderella Syndrome," believing that Prince Charming will suddenly appear and take away all of their problems, allowing them to live happily-ever-after. Searching for your Prince Charming (or trophy wife) is based on an illusion and illusions never last. Love is no shortcut to happiness, and marriage is no seat on the train to happily-ever-after.

People in their 30s often say that what they want out of a relationship now is different than what they wanted in their 20s. Why? Because in the intervening years they have taken the time to learn about themselves. Life experience has (hopefully) given them a far deeper understanding of what matters to them.

As one of three sisters, we all grew up with the idea that we would find someone who would take away our feelings of lack and insecurity. I was searching for someone who would love me enough for both of us. My parents put great emphasis on marriage and on finding the right man, far more than they did on our studies or careers. There was an implication that your fate was in the hands of the person you chose to marry.

1960s hit singer Jimmy Soul's philosophy on love was, "If you wanna be happy for the rest of your life, never make a pretty woman your wife." [37] My parents' philosophy was, "If you wanna be happy for the rest of your life, find a good provider who's Jewish, successful, and from a good family." I know, I know: it doesn't sound like my parents had much confidence in their daughters' ability to care for themselves without significant help.

Many of us are unaware of our false narratives, but as soon as you bring awareness to them, it is difficult for them to endure. Let's use this example of the belief that a partner will make you happy and fulfilled. Is this something you can picture yourself repeating to your daughter or even your younger self? Imagine your daughter growing up and passing on these pearls of wisdom: "But my Mom and Dad always said that a husband can fix everything!"

When I married Michael, I was convinced that I would magically be transported to a higher spiritual plane because he had been on a spiritual path since before he could read. I wasn't aware of my illusion until years into the marriage. Luckily, this wasn't a particularly damaging or problematic illusion, because it had to do with my own spiritual quest. It didn't skew who Michael was.

I didn't have an illusion about who I married, but an illusion about who I would be in the marriage.

For many individuals, their illusions have been more destructive.

Illusion: Getting married will make my life complete.
Many have the illusion that they will be totally fulfilled by newfound love. Women, in particular, tend to subscribe to the idea that marriage is a destination, an achievement to be ticked off a list of life goals and that once married, things will be perfect. I came across this humorous line: "He offered her the world, and she said, 'No thanks, I already have my own.'" The joke underscores the point that we should all be striving for our own full, independent, rich life. Marriage cannot fill that order, at least not on its own. This illusion is particularly unfair to men; why should one person be responsible for sustaining a world for two?

Illusion: It will always be romantic.
Romance is the hallmark of new love; that's part of the excitement. Both people in the relationship are hyper-focused in the beginning on pleasing each other, during the chase and excitement of the novelty. Both get used to this level of attention, and then when inevitably, as it must, energy shifts, they feel abandoned. Both partners end up losing appreciation for their partner and the relationship and therefore spend less time focusing on how to make each other feel special. Romance isn't just receiving flowers every Valentine's Day, or candlelight dinners. Romance is sparked by the more subtle things we tend to disregard when we're in a relationship for a long time, such as basic hygiene, and thoughtfulness toward your partner's desires.

Illusion: I will feel secure in the relationship once we are married.
Whatever you felt before marriage, you are going to feel it even more strongly after marriage. If you didn't feel secure while you were dating, then you may feel more insecure when you're married because marriage brings up a lot of issues and past insecurities.

Once you are in a committed relationship, spending more time together than apart, you become hyper-aware of each other's habits—from how you live, to what you eat, how you sleep, when you shower, and when or if you floss. Now all of that information isn't yours alone; it's now viewed and understood by the person you share your home with. That is why, for some, the first year of marriage is one of the most challenging.

Illusion: Having kids will ensure that we stay together forever.
This used to be far more prevalent than it is today. Most people are tuned in to the fact that committed relationships get thrown off balance when children come into the picture. Less attention is placed on each other's needs. Raising children takes a toll, no doubt about it. Just consider the fact that moms lose up to 700 hours of sleep in the first year of their child's life. [38]

I came across a story about a woman who wanted her husband to stop drinking, but she was afraid to confront him so she had a baby in hopes that the child would cause him to sober up. (That's a sobering thought.) This worked for a while until he started drinking again. But hope sprang eternal, and she had three more children before the marriage ended in divorce. She moved on, and over time met her second husband. Let's call him, "Phil Anderer." In an attempt to keep this husband faithful, she fell back on her old strategy and got pregnant. This had the desired effect for a little while, and when it stopped working, she tried the same band-aid approach two more times, until he left her for another woman. There are cheaper and less painful ways to stay together than giving birth seven times.

Buyer's Remorse

"When you stop expecting people to be perfect, you can like them for who they are." — Donald Miller [39]

The danger of illusions is that they lead to buyer's remorse. This is the point in the relationship when the sense of euphoria has dissipated, and the buyer wishes they could send back their order. Research shows that the intoxicating feeling we enjoy during the honeymoon phase of a relationship comes to us courtesy of a naturally-occurring chemical in the brain called dopamine. Its effect on our brains is similar to heroin and cocaine. Drugs that artificially raise dopamine levels put us at risk for addiction. They also cause horrible withdrawal symptoms when they're taken away. Sound familiar?

Like the high from drugs, the honeymoon phase will eventually wear off, which usually happens around the six-month mark. One person in the relationship suddenly begins to see flaws in his or her partner that they didn't notice before. Since that coincides with a diminishing sense of dopamine-enhanced pleasure, they think, "I'm not in love with this person anymore; the thrill is gone, so they can't be the one." But it could be a mistake to break up because sticking it out might allow a deeper love the chance to develop. The problem isn't your partner, but rather your unrealistic concept of who they should be, or even who you should be as a couple. At the beginning of a relationship, most people tend to de-emphasize the negative and overemphasize the positive. This imbalance is bound to rebalance. Negative feelings start to override the positive ones. Your focus becomes on changing your partner—except the person who needs changing is usually you.

When our partner isn't exactly who we pictured ourselves with in the long run, we have one foot in the relationship and one foot out. So naturally, when our illusion is shattered, we create a new one. It usually sounds like this: by staying in my current relationship, I am closing the door on the potential love of my life, who is undoubtedly waiting in the wings. This is another facet of the ego's version of love and keeps you from bettering and improving your relationship.

When feelings of buyer's remorse arise, remember this simple truth: if somebody has to change, it's probably you. As important as it is to find the right partner, it's more important to be the right partner.

Would you want to be married to you?

The Illusion of
All Illusions

Living in a cherished illusion is so common because we are so reliant on our five senses, yet so limited by them. The old adage is, "Seeing is believing," but we all know that things in life are often the opposite of what they appear to be. Believing is seeing, not the other way around.

KABBALISTIC PRINCIPLE:

We live in two realities: the 1% material world created by the illusion of our five senses, and the 99% dimension beyond our five senses.

· · · · · · · ·

According to Kabbalah, the material world represents 1% of reality. The 1% is the realm in which we are reactive, have only temporary joy or fulfillment, and often act as victims of our circumstances. It is a world of ups and downs. It nurtures a mindset where we are intent on achieving external goals.

The 99% realm, on the other hand, lies beyond what we can perceive. It's the spiritual realm in which we can make positive lasting change that will then transform our 1% world. When we are connected to the 99%, the Light is continuously flowing to us, and we live in consistent fulfillment. In the 99% realm, we are the cause, and in the 1%, we are the effect.

"Our senses are instruments that make us incapable of really understanding what is around us. What the eye sees is so little of what is out there. Our mind understands 1% of our psyche; our consciousness is limited to that 1% illusionary reality." — Rav Berg

Seeing is not believing. For instance, we know that infinitely small atomic particles contain vast resources of energy. Perfect examples of the 1% realm are electricity, the internet, gravity, and Wi-Fi signals. Even though we cannot see them, smell them, or touch them, we trust that they exist. We don't need to believe it, because we experience it working. The 99% realm is one of order and action rather than reaction. It is the origin from where everything in the 1% realm manifests. With the awareness that you are accessing 1% of the information around you, it becomes difficult to take what you see seriously. In those moments when things upset you, if you are able to say, "This is all an illusion," then you have begun the process of seeing the truth.

I am grateful that I didn't find a partner who fulfilled the cherished illusions of my younger, less spiritual self. One mistake people make is that they are focused on what they can see, like athletic ability, being a good dancer, or a stylish dresser. They aren't focusing on traits connected with the 99% spiritual realm, such as generosity, kindness, compassion, and thoughtfulness—not at first anyway. They tend to focus on traits connected with the 1% material realm, such as beauty, wealth, and power. At the time, these seem more important because they are the most obvious, which is precisely why they cannot be trusted. Because we are visceral beings, far too often we are limited by our five senses and end up with somebody who will fulfill us only in the short term. To find the right person, we must first become a person capable of "seeing" the 99% realm.

I have a childhood friend who, although she is a very caring person, is quick to anger. Every time her chronic anger flared up, instead of learning tools for how to transform her anger or work through it, she would resort to fantasies of her future life with a man who would take away her pain and never make her angry. So many times, I heard her say the words, "I just want to find that person who is going to love me unconditionally. Once I find him, I'm going to be happy." She believed this, and eventually, she found somebody who did love her deeply. He accepted her, anger and all. Now, of course, he wasn't perfect. Everyone has baggage, and he came with quite a bit—namely, a history of financial ups and downs. But even after becoming aware of his baggage, my friend said, "I don't care if he has money, I don't care if he's bankrupt, just as long as he loves me unconditionally."

Fifteen years later, she and her husband are still together (and her husband is still wildly in love with her), but anger still plays a significant role in her life. However, now the reasons for her anger have changed. She's angry about things she didn't realize she valued when she was younger because her illusions of romance got in the way. Yes, she did find unconditional love, but she now values stability, both financial and emotional, just as much.

This is a perfect example of what happens when our illusions fade. My friend believed that the love of a man would replace her anger with a sense of peace and stability. All of her anger and insecurities that were there before didn't disappear. She wanted someone to love her as she was instead of working on her flaws and anger issues. Those issues are her responsibility and only hers. It is simply not fair to make others responsible for our happiness. It is the ultimate setup for failure. So, my friend's anger continues because areas that you ignore will only grow worse.

Once, I was working with a student who was contemplating divorce. The more she told me about her relationship, the more perplexed I became. She told me she wanted to exit the marriage, yet in the same breath, she mentioned that she and her husband had just bought a house, were expecting another child, and were building a life together. Although her words were saying she wanted out, all of her actions indicated that she wanted to stay. We came to realize that in part, she still measured her relationship against the expectations she always had for marriage (her illusion). Therefore, she was having a hard time accepting the reality of what her life actually looked like. Despite being happy with her husband, she was still clinging to her unrealistic ideal.

Dispelling an illusion can be quite straightforward. When you feel dissatisfied, or find yourself blaming your partner for your needs not being met, this is the time to ask yourself, "What did I think marriage was going to bring me? And was that a realistic expectation?"

You might ask, what's left in a relationship once we clear away the illusions? The answer is different for everyone. If the relationship was based mostly on an illusion, then once the illusion is shattered, what you have left are broken pieces. If there are many positive aspects in the relationship, then once you have fewer unrealistic expectations, you can have a stronger relationship with your partner.

Chapter Eleven

Good Enough
Isn't Good Enough

"There is no passion to be found playing small —in settling for a life that is less than the one you are capable of living." — Nelson Mandela [40]

. . . .

Half-commitments make us feel emotionally drained and leave us in a place I call "The Almost." It's a place we've all been before: a land of good enough, close enough, and it's-just-so-comfortable. Many of us are living in the Almost in some area of our lives, but we will never be happy in our relationships, or our lives until we are fully committed to our unique purpose. When we commit to the wrong things or don't commit to anything, we find ourselves in our own Almost, living without any pressure to push ourselves forward towards something better. If you're going to train for a marathon, you're committing to running all 26.2 miles. At the 22-mile mark, you're not going to say, "This is pretty good. I think I'll stop." You didn't invest all that time and effort so you could *almost* finish. So why, when it comes to relationships, are we so quick to settle?

"The heart of misguided people is 'almost'." — King Solomon

Gabby is a bright, successful, beautiful woman in her 30s. When we discuss the man she's dating, however, she suddenly sounds like a different person. She seems doubtful about where she's going and unsure of what she wants. She doesn't want to move forward with her boyfriend, but she can't bring herself to leave him. When I asked her what they had in common, Gabby said, "He's a nice person, he's really trying to make the relationship work, and we see eye-to-eye in terms of our faith." I thought that sounded great, so I asked her what wasn't working. She said, "He still lives at home with his parents, he can't provide for himself, and when he does work, it's usually something I've set up for him." Gabby is in the Almost. A few things line up, the rest is disappointing, but maybe things will align better somewhere down the road.

After digging a bit deeper, we found that a big reason Gabby is staying in this relationship is that she thrives on feeling needed. Gabby doesn't think she's going to find anyone better, and if she does, would he ever need her as much? She is looking for her relationship to give her something only she can give herself: the knowledge that she is worthy and loved. Expecting a partner to meet needs that only you can meet for yourself is the beginning of settling, of living in the Almost.

KABBALISTIC PRINCIPLE:

To get out of the almost, you need to eradicate "good enough" and "close enough."

· · · · · · · ·

Jennie and Tom met in high school. He was four years older than she, popular and very handsome. Of all the girls he could have picked, and there were many, he chose her. She stayed with him even when she went off to college, and he did not. Tom didn't have high aspirations for himself, nor did he expect much from her, which represented a huge difference from the family she grew up in. Jennie had felt constant pressure from her successful parents, and two high-achieving older siblings. Her husband offered a welcome relief from that intensity. He gave her the unconditional acceptance and encouragement she lacked at home. It didn't matter that he was a functional drug addict.

As the years went by, Jennie inevitably began to feel a new kind of pressure. She was now supporting a household, which included Tom, a son, and Tom's growing drug problem. She finally put her foot down about the money he was spending on drugs and cut Tom off. Desperate, Tom set up a hidden camera in their bathroom, filmed Jennie taking showers, and sold the videos online to pay for his drug habit. The horror she felt upon this discovery finally shook her awake. It's an extreme example, but it illustrates an important point: Overlooking obvious problems and settling for less than what we want will have consequences down the line.

Why Do We Settle?

We can talk ourselves into, or out of, just about anything. A popular gambit is convincing ourselves that we're happy with the way things are. It looks like this:

- *"This isn't the relationship I wanted, but he's a nice guy, and he loves me."*
- *"This isn't the job I really wanted, but I am lucky to have one."*
- *"Everything is fine. Why do things have to change?"*

Even though we *know* we aren't truly happy, at least we're happy *enough*. Right? Sadly, no. This is the mantra of someone who is settling. Settling leads to only one place, a place where we finally become so miserable we are forced to change. The more you stay in this place, the harder it is to move from it. Whenever you settle, you always give up more than you expected.

If you choose a partner you feel you are settling for then you probably don't see them as your equal, which will open up an array of issues down the road. Choosing to settle is likely based on a fear of being alone, or on a belief that you don't deserve better. In the short-term, this may calm some fears and dispel loneliness, but over the long-term, they end up resenting and punishing their hapless spouses. No one benefits from settling. Resentment is a common theme among people who married their spouses because they were playing it safe. When you settle, you deprive yourself of the relationship you deserve, and you deprive your partner as well.

So You May Have Settled. Now What?

In relationships, if someone has settled, there is no incentive to desire more, and as a result, stagnation abounds. You are deep into the Almost, and to find your way out, you must recognize what you truly want, and then take steps to go after it. In times when you find yourself compromising, remember that isn't the path to any kind of true fulfillment.

There is a time for compromise, but you should never compromise your beliefs and certainly not sacrifice the love you deserve.

It takes courage to look at the state of your reality, both good and bad. If there's something about your relationship that isn't working for you now, understand that it can never work for you! What you find barely tolerable now, will be unbearable in 10 to 15 years.

I often hear women tell me they desperately want to leave their husband but that it's impossible for a long list of reasons. They have small children, and their spouse is the primary breadwinner, they're scared, where would they go, etc. This situation is not exclusive to women, either. Some men marry into a lot of money and leaving their wife would demand an enormous change in lifestyle. Fear of the unknown, or an even more uncomfortable situation, becomes the reason for staying in the relationship, which is a disaster in the making. Don't fall into the trap: take steps to either improve your situation or remove yourself from it. Yes, it might be scary, but remember that courage doesn't mean the absence of fear; it means acting in spite of it. Living courageously allows you to make changes now.

"Find joy in everything you choose to do. Every job, relationship, home. It's your responsibility to love it or change it." — Chuck Palahniuk

The Unexpected Guest

In his book, *The Secret,* my husband Michael shared the following tale that illustrates all too well the consequences of settling:

Hundreds of years ago, somewhere in Eastern Europe, there lived an impoverished couple. Josef and Rebecca's home was little more than a shack, and their only possession was a scrawny cow, from whose milk they fed themselves and earned a meager living. One afternoon Josef heard a knock on the door, and when he opened it, standing before him was the man widely recognized as the greatest kabbalist in the world, the Baal Shem Tov. He was accompanied by several of his students, who stood respectfully behind him.

"We've been traveling all day, may we join you for dinner?" asked the Baal Shem Tov.

"Of course," said Josef, showing them in. Rebecca was astonished and even a bit intimidated by the sudden appearance of the great kabbalist and his students.

"Very well then," said the Baal Shem Tov, glancing around. "But I have to tell you that my students and I are starving after our travels. We'd like some fine cuts of meat, some fresh vegetables, and, of course, some good wine. You can accommodate us, can't you?"

Josef hesitated before nodding enthusiastically. "Oh, yes," he said. "This is a great honor for us, let me just speak with my wife for a moment...."

He and Rebecca retired to a corner of the room. "What are we going to do?" Rebecca asked, anxiously. "How are we going to feed them? We have no meat or fresh vegetables, and the wine we drink isn't at all worthy of the Baal Shem Tov!" Josef thought for a moment. Then he said, "There's only one thing to do. I'll have to sell the cow to buy food. There's no time to waste!"

Within the hour, Josef returned with ingredients for the meal the Baal Shem Tov had requested, and Rebecca hurried to prepare it. As the great kabbalist began to eat, Josef and Rebecca were amazed by his capacity for food and drink. As soon as he finished one plate, he immediately called for more. He was a bottomless pit! Even his students were shocked, for they had never seen the Baal Shem Tov eat this way. Usually, he ate modestly and made sure that those around him were taken care of first. It was as if the Baal Shem Tov was trying to eat this poor couple out of house and home.

After downing the last morsel, the great man pushed his chair back from the table and rose to his feet. "That was delicious! Thank you very much," he said. "Now we have renewed energy for the road, so we will be on our way."

When the door had closed behind the departing visitors, Rebecca said, "Now we really have nothing, not even that scrawny cow! What are we going to do, Josef? We're going to starve!"

Unable to bear the sight of his weeping wife and with no idea what to do, Josef opened the door and stepped out into the cold night air. Soon he found himself wandering through the forest. How was he going to solve this terrible problem? He fell to his knees and began to pray. From the bottom of his heart, he asked for all the things he never had—not just for himself, but for his long-suffering wife who had sacrificed so much through the years.

Just then Josef heard a rustling in the branches behind him, and as he opened his eyes, he saw someone stagger towards him. It was an old man, well dressed but disheveled, who had obviously been drinking. When their eyes met, the old man's shone with happiness. "I'm so glad there's someone here," he said, slurring his words. "I don't want to die alone."

"Die?" said Josef, getting to his feet. "You're not going to die. You've just had a bit too much to drink."

But as Josef reached out to steady the newcomer, the old man slumped to the ground. As Josef knelt beside him, the man told a painfully sad story. He was very wealthy, but he had no family, and no friends with whom to share his good fortune.

"I'm sorry for your troubles, friend," Josef responded. "But it's cold out here, and you need a warm place to rest. Come home with me and my wife, and I will take care of you."

The old man just shook his head. "It's too late for that," he said. "But you've been so kind to me while seeking nothing in return. I can't remember the last time that happened, and I would like to repay your kindness. Here, take this."

But as he reached into the pocket of his coat, he began coughing. Then his face darkened, his eyes rolled up in his head, and he emitted a long, rattling sigh. Josef quickly bent over to help him, but sure enough, the man was dead. Curious about what the man was trying to give him, Josef gently reached into his pocket and found a map. When he returned the next day, he followed it deep into the forest where he discovered a buried treasure beyond anything he could have imagined.

Five years later to the day the Baal Shem Tov and his students were traveling along the road when a fine carriage passed them headed in the other direction. As the students glanced into its window, they were amazed to see Josef, the poor man who had struggled to provide them with dinner years before. Sitting beside him was his wife, and they both looked not just prosperous, but happy.

When the students turned to the Baal Shem Tov for some explanation, he only smiled calmly and said, "All along it was Josef s destiny to be joyful and fulfilled. But he never thought to ask for anything more than what he had. He would have been content to spend the rest of his life eking out a living from his one scrawny cow. That's why I had to help him get rid of it." To receive all the blessings that are destined for us, we need to believe we are deserving and not settle for anything less. When we settle, we stop asking, "What do I want?" We aren't meant to stay in place, no matter how good or not good it is. To correlate this to our lives today, the cow would be a mediocre relationship.

Ask yourself how you may be stuck in the Almost in some area of your life, whether it's in your relationship, or work, or family. Look for places where things are not great, but not terrible either, areas that are close enough. What can you do to make yourself uncomfortable—not for its own sake, but in order to create the relationship you desire?

Chapter Twelve

Distinguishing Between
Fact & Fiction

A friend of ours who we don't see very often joined Michael and me for dinner, when our second son, Josh, came up in conversation. Michael and I had been talking about moving to New York, and we were explaining that the move would be complicated by the additional support Josh needs in terms of therapy and overall assistance. Our friend, who has known Josh since birth, asked, "What do you mean? Why would Josh need therapy?" I replied, "You know he has Down syndrome." Our friend's mouth dropped open. He had no idea.

After a brief pause, he said, "You just don't wear it."

It was the biggest compliment he could have paid us. Why? Because when things happen in our lives, we tend to wear them. We wear our emotions on our faces and in our bodies. Feelings of betrayal, resentment, and sadness become the lines on our face, the foundation of our identity, and ultimately the energy with which we express ourselves. We become the character we've chosen in whatever tragedy/comedy/drama we've agreed is taking place. But this isn't always the case. Michael and I don't act like we have a child with a disability or treat him like he has one. In no way do we feel like victims, we just see our son.

The good news is that you don't have to wear anything you don't want to wear. How you choose to look at what happens to you determines your happiness. And things will happen. How you choose to experience them is what matters. This is how we begin to embrace what is. And begin to experience life as we are meant to live it.

The Stories We Tell Ourselves

"Those who do not have power over the story that dominates their lives, the power to retell it, rethink it, deconstruct it, joke about it, and change it as times change, truly are powerless, because they cannot think new thoughts." — Salman Rushdie [42]

Stories are an essential aspect of every culture. We enjoy theater, curling up with a good book, going to a musical, the ballet, or the opera. No matter the medium, any work of art tells a story. Owen Flanagan, a leading consciousness researcher, writes that "Evidence strongly suggests that humans in all cultures come to cast their own identity in some sort of narrative form. We are inveterate storytellers." [43]

It is in our nature to tell stories, and to take pleasure from hearing them, but sometimes the stories in our heads—even the ones we aren't aware of—create an unhealthy disconnect between us and those who are most meaningful to us.

KABBALISTIC PRINCIPLE:

The Zohar explains that what we think we
see is not always what is. We cannot grasp what
is happening at a single moment if all we are
taking into account is the present.

. . . .

There is no rulebook for life, so we create our own rules and stories based on what we see, both good and bad. The lady who cut you off in traffic (*troll!*); the parking attendant who always gives you the worst spot (*ogre!*); the boss who gives you too much work (*six-eyed monster!*) To some extent, we're all guilty of storytelling, because it gives us a false sense of control and keeps us from owning our power. Thinking, "My boss is a monster," is an easier excuse as to why you dislike your job than actually having a constructive discussion that would address your needs and issues. Some stories serve us, and some stories don't, but once we realize we are creating these stories, we are in a better position to separate fact from fiction. If you say anything enough times, you'll begin to believe it. Hitler's rise to power and his distorted belief in a "pure" gene pool was nothing more than a story, which is a perfect example of the terrible consequences of stories, and a testament to their power.

The following are examples of negative stories that keep us from creating the real change we crave:

- *"My husband had an affair. I'm going to divorce him, and then I'm never going to find love again."* Creates the story: I am unlovable.
- *"My mother loved my sister more."* Creates the story: I am not as worthy of love as others are.
- *"I was humiliated by my teacher, repeatedly, in front of the entire class for all of 5th grade."* Creates the story: I'm stupid. Anytime I put myself out there, I'm going to be humiliated.

We create fiction instead of relating facts so that we don't have to confront difficult circumstances and emotions. Here is an example of what Fact versus Story can look like in a relationship:

FACT – "My partner is being distant."
STORY – "My marriage is over."

Saying your marriage is over, instead of paying attention to why your partner is distant, is perhaps a less painful alternative to learning what the actual problem is. It might even feel easier than having to do the work of fixing it—at the moment, anyway. It is tricky to decipher at first, but once you do, you'll be able to make real, lasting change because you can't rewrite a story without healing old patterns and behaviors.

Your past experiences are stored in your memory like movies, each with its own stellar cast of heroes and villains, perhaps one or two not-so-fitting love interests, and then finally "the One." They can be dramas, comedies, thrillers, and maybe even horror films. I know I've had my share of all of them. Subconsciously we do everything we can to support the story playing in our head. We find and cast co-stars, and we construct the ending we need to support our beliefs and insecurities. Soon we've got front-row seats to a major motion picture.

Speaking of genres, have you ever noticed that romantic comedies usually end with a wedding, while dramas typically begin with a married couple? We can weigh our lives against what we see in pop culture, but the problem is we don't get a script. We don't know what genre we're in, and we don't have a plot laid out that helps us find our way through our challenges. Although we tend to live out scripts that we think are created for us, actually we are the screenwriters. We write our own narrative. This is good news because it means we can rewrite it anytime. As such, this is the responsibility we need to take: rewriting our scripts through shifting our consciousness. Thoughts are just thoughts and can be changed. As kabbalist Rav Berg said, "Consciousness is everything." Our thoughts dictate what is.

Rewriting the Script

"Failure is part of the process of success. People who avoid failure also avoid success." — Robert Kiyosaki [44]

A woman grew up in the Midwest surrounded by men who rarely expressed a full range of emotions. Anger, sure, but not sensitivity, anxiety, or vulnerability. She spent her entire dating life believing that men just weren't connected to their feelings. She found comfort in the stoic attitude of her family members and the men she knew, equating it with safety, dependability, and strength. After dating this kind of man for years, she started to find holes in her plotline. She couldn't find fulfillment in these relationships and she never knew where she stood with them because these men weren't emotive. She mistook familiarity with safety and found herself feeling the exact opposite, unprotected. Once she realized how she was searching for the wrong archetype, she made a conscious effort to be open to men who were the opposite of the ones in her story. Now she's in her third year of marriage to a very emotionally available and secure man.

When you choose to spend the rest of your life with someone, make sure that they're aware of the key plot points in your movie, at least as you understand them, and make yourself just as familiar with theirs. The stories of our lives hold some critical data. By sharing them, you are releasing the false thoughts and feelings, real or imagined, that you have about your life experiences.

If, for instance, someone lost their mother at a very young age, they may believe love is fleeting, and that although they can fall in love, it won't last forever. With stories like this in our heads, we may end up pushing love away or putting our partners in untenable situations just to prove our stories right.

Once you choose the person that you want to spend your life with, it won't serve you to only let them see some aspects of your psyche. This isn't an easy process, but it is a necessary one. In order to be vulnerable with each other, we need to be open, honest, and accepting of ourselves, or we will never achieve true intimacy. There are times when we regret the choices we've made and may experience feelings of self-hatred. We then may begin to hide aspects of our past and personality, and this can be detrimental.

During a pre-marriage counseling session with a couple two months prior to their big day, the groom revealed he had been having major doubts about getting married. He felt he needed space from his fiancée and wanted to spend more time alone. He was afraid to tell her this because he didn't want to hurt her feelings, and also because he felt she wouldn't understand. He had created a movie where she wasn't the one for him, and he wasn't ready to get married.

His desire not to hurt her feelings led him to not share his own. This created a gap between them, leaving him feeling distant enough to question whether he should be getting married. I encouraged him to tell her how he was feeling so she could be a part of his process. It was uncomfortable and potentially damaging, but at this point, what did he have to lose? As hard as some of this was for her to hear, once he started sharing his innermost feelings it became apparent to both of them that the claustrophobic feelings he was experiencing were based on his own intimacy issues, and had nothing to do with her at all—intimacy issues that would surely have come up early in their marriage. I'm happy to say they both walked down the aisle, he with a clear conscience and she with an open heart. Their honest exchange paved the way to successfully navigate the difficult conversations that inevitably arise in marriage.

I'm often asked, "How vulnerable do I really need to be in my relationship? How much do I need to divulge to my partner?" My response: "Tell them everything!" I am often met with a look of shock and disbelief. Secrets and lies have a nasty habit of breeding more secrets and lies which take a terrible toll on intimacy. The alternative is full transparency. It's cleaner, simpler, and its byproduct is trust. Problems arise not because we are unaware of our partner's story or their past, but because we are not aware of the stories in our own minds.

Kara and Saul were a model couple; all of their friends looked up to them as a shining example of a happy marriage. They had been married for eight years when Kara unexpectedly became pregnant with their third child, just three months after the birth of their second. The arrival of a third child threw an already hectic family life into turmoil. Now they had a six-year-old, a one-year-old, and a new baby who turned out to be allergic to just about everything, and as such, was constantly fussy and crying, often covered in rashes, and plagued with gas and digestive issues. Kara, who was breastfeeding, went on a restricted diet because if she ate foods outside a very short list, the baby became ill.

Needless to say, this was a trying time for Kara and Saul as a couple. They were exhausted, frustrated, worried about their son's health, and to add to the tension, they stopped being intimate—emotionally and physically. They had always honored weekly date nights, usually going out to a restaurant to unwind and reconnect. But now Kara couldn't eat out, and they were reluctant to saddle a babysitter with a colicky baby. Kara was so busy with the children that she had no energy left for Saul, so she was only peripherally aware that he had been steadily withdrawing from her. She started to create a story in her head where she saw Saul not as a partner, but a selfish, distant, unsupportive bystander.

Saul had his own elaborate story, which cast the blame on Kara for all of their misfortunes, because after all, in his mind, she was the irresponsible one for getting pregnant again (even though she had been on birth control). It was at this time that Saul reconnected with an old high school friend on Facebook who was recently divorced. Saul found himself looking forward to her messages, checking them several times a day. He knew it wasn't right, but when he imagined bringing it up with Kara, he could imagine his wife's reaction: "How dare you! I am up all night with this baby, taking care of your other two children, I can't eat any of the things I love, and you have the nerve to pretend that you flirting with a girl from high school is somehow my fault? This is your problem. Get it together!"

He wasn't prepared to have this conversation and instead, convinced himself that nothing was really going on. But something was. Now Saul had a secret, and a secret is the first step in betrayal. Saul's emotional affair spiraled into a physical one. He was so ashamed that he eventually confessed this to Kara. Through continued talks and a lot of effort, Saul and Kara were able to rebuild their marriage, but not all couples are so lucky. They had both created victim stories, where each blamed the other for the state of their lives. The affair, in their case, was a wake-up call, showing them how much had come between them, how they had lost their friendship, and no longer made each other a priority.

They promised that they would always disclose their feelings no matter what and would not be afraid of perceived consequences. Now they know the damage of holding things back. Saul wasn't a distant, unsupportive person—he was going through a stressful time, as was she. Kara wasn't an irresponsible person, and sometimes things just happen that are out of our control. Had they turned toward each other early on, the stories in their heads might not have gotten so far along. But as it turned out, the hardship they suffered eventually made their marriage even stronger because they agreed to rely on each other in the future when difficulties would arise.

Very often, we're committed to being the victim in a situation. But how do we get past this and not allow our grievances to become our story of victimization? Typically, when you become upset, do you ask yourself, "Who is responsible for this?" (More than likely, the answer is you.) When we perceive that the cause lies with another person, then we think the solution to that hurt is also reliant on another person, and therefore, we look outside of ourselves for the solution. This approach doesn't work.

To stop playing the victim in your stories, you must be willing to own your choices and their consequences. As long as you are unwilling to take responsibility for your life, grievance stories will be an intrinsic part of your day-to-day existence. Over time you may lose the ability to tell fact from fiction. Once you become aware of your stories, you can find a new outlet for your creativity.

Rethink Moment

Next time you find yourself creating a story, take pause and ask yourself, "Am I jumping to conclusions?" Here are two steps that will help you begin to unravel your stories and rewrite new narratives.

Step 1: Is what you see based on something real or stems from a false belief? Ask yourself:

• Am I addressing facts, or am I creating a story?

• Do I have an ulterior motive for seeing things this way?

• Am I making assumptions about someone else's behavior?

Step 2: Don't hesitate to ask questions of other people when you need clarification. There's no such thing as a dumb question. You're gathering information so you can see things for what they are.

• Why did you say that? I am confused by what just happened, maybe you could help me sort it out.

Our stories are nothing more than illusions of control. While we all wish to have more control over our lives—from finding the perfect house, to getting a great mortgage rate, to landing the dream job—in truth, the result is never really up to us. There is a lot we do not see and do not know.

For thousands of years, kabbalists have been keenly aware of just how little control we really have. We don't control when we were conceived, when we're born, or when we die. This is a fundamental understanding we all know. The same principle applies to everything we experience, meaning we have just as little control over the middle as we do in the beginning or the end. We can create a business, but we don't know if it will boom. We can create a child, but we don't know if the child will thrive.

We cannot control the world around us, but we can control our reaction to it.

Instead of creating stories that give us a false feeling of authority over the many things that are beyond us, we can focus instead on two things we can control: our thoughts and our actions.

Chapter Thirteen

Me, Myself and I, I, I, I, I...

**"Enough about me, what about you...
What do YOU think of me?" — Bette Midler, *Beaches* [45]**

. . . .

Why do people who love one another get into painful and often hugely destructive fights? The answer is contained in one word, and a short word at that: ego. Ego is what leads us to believe that we have the answers to our partners' perceived shortcomings. The ego doesn't like to feel slighted and, before you know it, you will constantly be feeling as if your partner 'never listens' to you. Instead of thinking about the thoughts and needs of others, we think, "You're not making me happy. You're not fulfilling my needs." Ego tells us that, "You're wrong, and I'm right." We may think we're in opposition to those around us when our real foe is our ego.

Ego has many definitions. In Eastern philosophy, the ego refers to the self, the "I am." Freud initially understood ego to mean a sense of self as well, but then revised it to refer to that part of the psyche involved in issues like judgment, tolerance, control, planning, defense, and memory. [46] The dictionary defines ego as self-esteem or self-importance and that which gives one a sense of personal identity. Ego helps us organize our thoughts and make sense of the world around us. Ego can work for us (an "ego boost" gives us encouragement and spurs us on), or against us (a "bruised ego" often leads to reactive behavior).

Your real enemy is never another person. It is your ego.

. . . .

Kabbalist Rav Ashlag teaches that our ego is not connected to our true essence, but rather is an aspect of our human nature, validating for us that it's okay to treat another without respect and human dignity. Our egos are very caught up in what we think, know, and need, and we can get very comfortable seeing the world through this lens, which unfortunately doesn't consider the needs and feelings of others. There's no point in berating ourselves for being ruled by the ego at times, but once we know the beast we're dealing with, we can find ways to tame it.

Many spiritual traditions focus on defusing the ego. Successfully sublimating the ego is known as nirvana, enlightenment, and, kabbalistically is referenced as being one with the Light, the force of kindness and sharing. Spiritually minded people tend to associate the ego with something unhealthy, with narcissism or an inflated sense of self-worth. The ego seeks to defend our sense of identity in a myriad of ways. In synchrony with Freud's understanding, Kabbalah identifies ego with defense mechanisms like denial, delusions, displacement, over-compensation, projection, rationalization, reactive behavior, and repression.

The ego always has an agenda, and whenever that agenda isn't being met, we tend to get angry and blame someone, often our partner. As we move into a love relationship, the ego is bound to show up in ways that surprise us, which is one reason why relationships offer such an excellent opportunity for spiritual growth.

Under the Influence (of Your Ego)

The ego is very clever. It's adept at leading us to believe that we need to push our own agenda forcefully and continuously, or we will suffer some great loss: we might be disrespected, threatened, or ostracized. These beliefs feel very real, yet the alternately aggressive and fearful approach they inspire is not going to get us far in our relationships, so we need to see past the ego's agenda. For instance, whether or not you agree, you still have to respect your partner. When you do not see eye-to-eye, your ego will step in and tell you the other person is trying to control you, or do you wrong. If you take your ego seriously, it will then lead to defensive behavior that will only exacerbate an argument.

Certainly, you can offer your opinion, but nobody has to accept it. This doesn't mean your opinion isn't valid, but at that moment, the other person just may not be ready to hear it.

You want to strive to hear each other, but understand that ultimately each partner has a choice to make, right or wrong; how you react to it will affect whether or not you remain friends in the process.

As much as you may wish for your opinion to prevail, everybody has their own process to go through. (The old saying "You can be right, or you can be married" comes to mind here.)

The biggest obstacle to a successful, happy, and fulfilling relationship is ego. Ego-driven love is selfish love. Ego distorts reality, causing us to see others as threats or objects to manipulate. When we live our lives guided by our egos, we don't see the good in others. Much of what we see in the 1% is an illusion painted by ego.

Ego sounds like this:
- *"I need to be right, which means you must be wrong."*
- *"If you disagree, I'm justified in becoming angry or annoyed."*
- *"I become envious when someone has more than I do, so I talk badly about them and take pleasure in their misfortunes."*
- *"I dismiss people who I deem insignificant as unworthy of my time and love."*

Nobody wants to find out that they think this way. But be honest with yourself, how much of this rings true to you?

The ego is tricky because it is often disguised as self-righteousness or discernment, but we can learn to detect its presence and take steps to minimize its influence. Nothing transforms a person more consistently than calming their ego. When we act with kindness instead of reacting to ego, we can see the world from the other person's point of view. By doing so, we break down the walls of prejudice to find we are all connected.

Unity is the outcome of diminishing our ego. In unity, there is no division between people, and we can feel their pain as if it were our own. This is how we begin to break the grip of ego and move from "Me" to "We." This isn't easy. Ego is powerful. But reducing its influence is one of the most positive things you can do for yourself and your partner. We may feel satisfied with our relationships, but a far richer experience can be had as soon as we see the world beyond the lens of our egos.

On the night of December 25th, 1776, General George Washington crossed the icy Delaware River, leading his troops towards Trenton, New Jersey, where Hessian soldiers were celebrating Christmas. They had let their guard down, confident that the beleaguered Continental army posed no immediate threat. During the Christmas celebration, a spy gave Johann Rall, the officer in charge of the Hessians, a note revealing that General Washington was much closer than they knew. Lulled by a false sense of security, Rall tucked the note in his pocket and continued with the holiday merriment. Later that night his forces were attacked and decisively defeated. When Colonel Rall was killed retreating from battle, the note was found unopened in his coat pocket. [47]

This story is an example of the way ego deceives us. Egos are infamous for convincing us that we know the truth, that we are headed in the right direction, that we don't need anyone's help. Many of us let our ego dictate our lives, giving us a false sense of fulfillment, encouragement, self-righteousness, and even worse, control. However, ego cannot bring you closer to others. Ego supports a feeling of superiority, which creates disconnection. One of our big problems in life, and in relationships, is the fact that we're so sure we know what we know. Countless petty arguments begin with what one partner "knows" and will inevitably continue because the other partner "knows" the opposite.

I know how, what, when, why, or where it is supposed to happen.

All of this knowing comes from ego. It can come from the simplest, mundane thing to something of great importance. For example, I wake up in the morning, "I know" it's going to be an effortless morning, and so I only allow for the 20 minutes of driving time that it should take to get to the gym. But then a garbage truck blocks the street, and it takes at least 10 minutes to clear. Naturally, I'm upset, because I know how it was supposed to go and this wasn't part of the plan.

Let's look at this on a larger scale, upon entering a marriage, we have an idea of what the rest of our life will be. For instance, after two years we are going to start a family, have three healthy children, and we're going to be very happy together. But if things don't go according to this plan, this person will most likely become disappointed, perhaps even devastated, because they were so sure that they *knew* what was going to happen. Our lives are built around expectations. When things don't work out as planned, we often blame the person closest to us, and our partner bears the brunt.

When Shakespeare wrote the words in Macbeth, *"It is a tale / Told by an idiot, full of sound and fury / Signifying nothing"* he was describing life, but he might just as well have been referring to the ego.

People often get confused about the differences between the ego and having certainty. Ego is associated with an unwillingness to learn, with being close-minded, with unbridled and unfounded confidence. When I speak of certainty, I'm talking about placing my complete conviction in the Creator. Certainty is the consciousness of being open to possibilities and new ways of thinking. Ego refers to rigidity, inflexibility, and control.

Certainty is trusting the process of life; the ego wants to control that process.

I'm all for planning, and I find great value in it. But at the end of the day, we need to remember that we don't know how, what, when, why, or where our plan is meant to manifest. By letting go of your predisposed ideas of what's supposed to happen, you also release the traps of disappointment, anger, and pain, and open up to the divine plan. By all means, direct your energy and effort towards creating what you desire, but try to let go of the way you think that should unfold.

"Restriction doesn't mean giving up what you want; it means letting go of the way you think you're going to get it." — Rav Berg

Once you've done your best, let it go. You can't dictate the outcome. Life may have other plans in store for you—which may be far greater than the one you're pursuing.

Gimme, Gimme: Ego-Based Love

The wisdom of Kabbalah teaches us to be wary of feelings that seem intoxicating. All romances start out this way, like a thousand flashbulbs all going off at once to indicate that you've found the missing piece of your emotional jigsaw puzzle. This is a natural state to be in at the onset of budding love. It's important to have the awareness that love needs to grow beyond this into a deeper, spiritual love that is, at its foundation, based on sharing and human dignity. When you feel euphoric, but you don't grow, that love remains a love solely based in the realm of ego, which has an inevitable expiration date. So what may have started out as a version of love, eventually becomes love's polar opposite.

We're accustomed to thinking of love almost exclusively in terms of self-centered needs: what I feel, what I want. We think we're nourishing our relationship with acts of love, and we are until we start to count those actions. Once we begin to tally how much we're doing for our partner and how much they're doing for us, we've started keeping score. Scorekeeping gives us a reason to stop giving to our partner, and for a relationship to grow, there always has to be a push to give.

We have a list in our mind of all the things we've done and sacrificed for our partner, all the opportunities we've lost because of them, all the could-haves, and should-haves.

I love my husband very much. But imagine if I'm always thinking about the unbelievable things I've done for him and all the ways I've stretched and gone above and beyond. If we really love somebody, we love their essence. We love their mere existence, not what they do for us. When we truly love someone, there's no scorekeeping.

In the beginning of my marriage, when we used to have arguments, I kept score. My favorite mantra was, "He won last time, and now, in fairness, it's my turn to win." That's what happens for a lot of couples when they argue, and it sets you up for a really negative outcome.

"If winning isn't everything, why do they keep score?" — Vince Lombardi [48]

For our relationships to thrive, we need to get the third party—our ego—out of the bedroom.

The foundation of a strong relationship that isn't solely for mutual benefit isn't found in the material world. It's about receiving what the Creator intends for you, which is infinite joy and fulfillment. In this kind of relationship, it is more important to give than to receive. Too often love is recognized as the good feelings we receive from another person. Over time the expectation that your partner's purpose is to make you feel good creates an imbalance, allowing the getting to take precedence over the giving. Ego-based love places our needs ahead of others. It leads us to ask, "What am I getting?" rather than the infinitely more important question, "What am I giving?"

When we move into the mindset of giving, we move beyond the realm of ego-based love. When we make the happiness and wellbeing of our partner a priority, the ego relinquishes control. We allow our true nature, the source of unconditional love, to take over.

Part Three

We
May cause profound love stories

Chapter Fourteen

Elevating Love

The purpose of love is to connect us to the divine Light, which is endless and more powerful than anything we can even imagine. This is something to look forward to and to work towards.

Love which is based on sharing is powerful and lasting. And the more you share, the greater your capacity to give. The difference between ego-based love and unconditional love is that the latter has the ability to grow endlessly, always creating a deeper and stronger bond. Unconditional love is not about power, wealth, or self-esteem, nor is it about what you get or do not get. To love unconditionally is to value the characteristics in a person that are a manifestation of his or her core self. The only expectations are to be heard, respected, and treated with human dignity.

Unconditional love is the foundation of a happy relationship, and it is not only attainable, it is a birthright for absolutely everybody.

KABBALISTIC PRINCIPLE:

To love unconditionally means you love the
person simply because they exist.

. . . .

"I love you just the way you are." These are more than the lyrics to a Billy Joel [49] song we hear at weddings, or a phrase we use at home or with our closest friends. But what does it really mean? Does it mean that we love someone for absolutely no reason? Does it mean we love them without justification? Does it mean that we love them no matter what they may do?

I find it amusing when parents of young children say, "I love my child, unconditionally." It's relatively easy to love toddlers unconditionally because they haven't learned to talk back. But when they become teenagers they've not only mastered that skill, but they have unflattering opinions that they don't hesitate to express, and they're subject to a stormy sea of mood swings. You may wonder where that unconditional love went when your teenager finally pushes you beyond your breaking point. Unconditional love doesn't go anywhere. It just becomes a little less accessible. After all, the soul of your child is the same at 15 as it was at two.

It's easier to love unconditionally when you remember that we are all in the middle of our stories as they're unfolding. "Human beings are works in progress that mistakenly think they're finished," says Harvard professor Daniel Gilbert, author of *Stumbling on Happiness.* [50]

Most of us assume that we are going to have a healthy child, or that our partner will take care of us in sickness and in health. When these assumptions turn out to be false, we are forced to reconsider what we're basing our love on. In these moments, it becomes clear that our love is conditional or unconditional depending on how we respond to these dramatic changes of circumstance. For instance, a married couple may feel happy until the husband loses his six-figure income. This is an opportunity to embrace change. If you are going to be partners, this means you're partners through the ups *and* the downs. That requires being willing to face and overcome the challenges together that will inevitably occur.

It's hard not to react when your partner is skillfully pushing your hot buttons or screaming that he hates you. It's hurtful to be on the receiving end of this. The road back to connecting and to the unconditional love you feel for them is to see things from their perspective. How are they feeling right now, beyond the obvious anger?

What are they frustrated about? What hurt or anxiety is prompting them to lash out at you this way? Once again, we're talking about a simple shift away from "me," to "him" or "her."

No good ever comes from reacting to someone else's bad behavior.

If you can maintain your equanimity instead of losing it, you can find a way to feel empathy for their situation and understand why they are projecting their anger on you. Get in touch with unconditional love by disconnecting from your partner's bad behavior. Remove your ego from the fray, and reconnect to the essence of the person you fell in love with.

Set Point

A way to jumpstart removal of the ego is to place emphasis on the positive. You can change your relationship's set point, similar to the set point approach to weight loss, which is a popular theory stating that the body has a set weight it tries to maintain, no matter how much you diet, and so your body has a strong tendency to hover at that weight. Only by resetting your body's metabolism, typically via exercise, can dieting help you lose weight for good.

It's similar in marriage. Once your marriage gets set at a certain degree of positivity, it will take far more negativity to harm your relationship than if your set point were lower. Most marriages start off with such a high positive set point that it is hard for either partner to imagine the relationship derailing. It takes maintenance to sustain your positive set point. Sometimes your negative feelings will override your positive sentiments about your partner, and resentment can build up to the point that friendship becomes more and more of an abstraction.

When you're in that place, sometimes even words said in a neutral tone of voice are taken in a negative way. For example, if one partner says, "You're not supposed to set the thermostat at that temperature." The response from the other partner might be, "Don't tell me what to do. I read the manual." When you're starting at a low point, then things are easily misunderstood.

131

"I can't find my car keys! Where did you put them?" A negative set point response might be, "You're always losing things! Don't blame me, go look for them!"

I ask couples on the verge of separation or divorce, "Why did you fall in love in the first place," or "How did you feel on your wedding day?" Often, they don't know and can't even recall ever loving this person. When you focus on the negative, you 'set' your relationship as such. As an exercise for one week, try to be extra thoughtful when it comes to your partner. Ignore your inclination to say negative things and watch what happens. Take it a step further and add in a sprinkle of consideration and pepper it with benefit of the doubt. This will shift the dialogue in your head and, consequently, the actions that follow.

In marriages with high positive set points, husbands and wives share a deep sense of purpose; they support each other's hopes and aspirations. Dr. John Gottman, a psychology professor who specializes in marital stability, has found successful couples say or do at least five positive things for each negative interaction with their partner. [51]

Two Steps to Loving Unconditionally

Most of us are pretty far away from consistently giving love unconditionally. Here are good strategies for bridging that gap.

- **Step 1: Let your partner have their journey**. When we judge our partners, we're not supporting their journey. Unconditional love means letting those you love walk their own path. This may sometimes mean letting them hit rock bottom, as hard as that is to witness. We simply have to love them through it.

The first time I experienced this concept in a profound way was with my father. I have fond memories of us walking along the streets of Laguna Beach, a quaint, artsy beach community in Southern California. At the time, I was suffering from anorexia, and my frail body was as starved for

132

nutrients as my heart was for unconditional love. I was lost, weary, voiceless, and plagued by doubts and fears, but my father simply walked by my side, strong, silent, and most definitely present.

My father never pressed me for answers about why I was starving myself, nor did he ever beg me to eat. He never inquired about my caloric intake, nor did he try to force me to see what I was doing to myself. While this could be read as a lack of interest or concern on my father's part, I knew he was coming from a place of love. How? Because I never felt judged by him; I just felt him there, ready to pick me up if I were to fall. He was well aware of the seriousness of my anorexia, but I think he knew that if he pressed me on my eating habits, I would just retreat deeper into myself. I felt great comfort in my dad's presence. He was my rock. He never tried to control me or the situation. He just loved me through it. Although this seems like a simple thing, it's far from easy to do.

I was determined to hike through the Grand Canyon, and my father agreed to accompany me. I'm pretty sure no doctor would have cleared a diabetic (my father) or an anorexic (me) for a strenuous trip like this. I filled a backpack with two 1.5 liter bottles of water, an energy bar, and some dried fruit. We exerted so much energy that day I didn't urinate once, and my collarbones were literally reshaped by the weight of my backpack. I carry those dents to this day. My father had his own struggles. The trek down the canyon is straight downhill to the Colorado River, which means the trek back is a pure ascent; this became a huge obstacle for him. We needed to stop frequently on the way back as my father grappled with severe cramping in his legs and blisters on his feet.

I wasn't sure we'd make it out of the canyon before dusk, which would have been bad news because we had no backup plan. No tents, jackets, blankets, or extra food and water. If you look up how to prepare for hiking the Grand Canyon, one of the first things it says in big red letters is **"The difference between a great adventure in the Grand Canyon and a trip to the hospital (or worse) is up to you. DO NOT attempt to hike from the rim to the river and back in one day, especially during the months of May to September."** Of course, without having read this back then, that's precisely what we did. By the time we finally, miraculously, exited the Grand Canyon I looked behind me, the sun had just set, and I saw a pack of highly reflective coyote eyes staring at me. We were lucky to make it out of that canyon for many reasons. But there we were, at each other's side. He joined me on my soul-searching journey all the way down to the Colorado River and back up again, in one day.

It's interesting to consider love and control, two strong forces, and how they compete with each other.

We often try to control the ones we love, but by controlling them, we are not truly loving them.

Love and control cannot exist in the same space. When we try to exercise control, we're making the interaction about ourselves, our desired outcome, our advice, our opinion. My father never made my eating disorder about him. He remained true to himself, and therefore to me, as well.

My mother was an indomitable force, always checking in on me, asking about my weight and what I had eaten. Her constant worry was if I would survive, and her consistent questions were, "Are you hungry?" and "Did you eat today?" To which I answered, "no" and "yes," respectively, when truth be told, it was the other way around.

An eating disorder is a very lonely and isolating experience; it feels like a prison. This cell I had created for myself felt even more confining due to my mother's worry. As a mother myself, I now understand her worry, but it was my father who provided me the freedom to simply be. I am sure he was just as frightened as my mom, but he never lectured me. For a man who knew how to deliver a strong message, this was an amazing restriction on his part.

The secret to loving unconditionally is learning to go against your own nature.

My father gave me the freedom to figure things out for myself. He was a warm breeze through the open window of my prison cell.

Both my father, the rock of my childhood, and my husband, the steadfast man of my present, know how to simply stand by my side. While my husband is quite different from my father in many ways, they both have remarkable hearts, and when they love you, they love you forever.

- **Step 2: Let go of judgment.** I spoke with someone recently who was disappointed with all of her relationships—with her friends, her fiancée, and her work colleagues. She said she was always being let down. I asked her, "Are all of these things you expect from other people also things that you are giving to them?" The answer was no. She was far too busy judging them. If you are judging, you aren't motivated to give. Unconditional love has no conditions, and therefore no judgments.

When my father was diagnosed with a benign brain tumor, without doing any research, he decided immediately to have it removed. This was a fear-based reaction, and I found myself judging my father's choice. Although he had been so enlightened during my health scare, twenty years later, he acted very differently when faced with his own. The more fearful he became, the less open-minded he was about finding ways to get better. And the less supportive I felt like being.

I was disappointed by how I was responding to my father, so I took it as an opportunity to check myself. Regardless of whether I agreed with his decisions or not, I still needed to practice unconditional love. I learned a very valuable lesson here: it's easier to feel empathy for others when you approve of their choices and actions. That's nice, but it's not unconditional love.

Unconditional love involves letting go of judgment, control, and self-interest.

Selfless Love

The Zohar states, "As we act in this world, so we awaken acts from above." Rav Berg often said, "The Light is your shadow." Meaning, the way we behave is what the Light mimics. The way I behave towards others is how the Light behaves towards me. Kabbalah explains that every instance of happiness, whether the small satisfaction of a task well done at work or the great joy that accompanies the birth of a child, has its source in a universal energy.

The Arvei Nachal, a great 18th-century kabbalist, taught that when two people achieve a bond so close that each puts the well-being of the other above his own, the Creator will set aside all of His other concerns in order to shine Light upon them.

Generosity is a significant factor in strengthening every relationship. What does it mean to be generous? In the context of friendship, it means to be the giver and not the receiver, which can be expressed in many ways. For some, it's remembering birthdays, or throwing a celebratory dinner party. For me, it's inspiring people to live their greatest potential. It's up to you to find your own ways to be generous to your friends, but finding the balance between what you give and what you receive is essential to your happiness, health, and well-being.

Part of finding this balance sometimes entails making a sacrifice for somebody. Kabbalistically, the most meaningful giving is not what comes easily — cash from the wealthy or clothing when you're cleaning out your closet. A meaningful gift requires sacrifice — giving up something valuable to you in order to help someone else.

Do you make sacrifices for the people you love?

There are two types of sacrifice: healthy and unhealthy. Unhealthy appears to work at first because it's a quick solution. Unhealthy sacrifices are often well intentioned but don't work over the long-term.

Healthy sacrifices are when we are willing to sacrifice fear for love, independence for intimacy, defense for joy, and resentment for forgiveness.

Studies show that our own happiness is often boosted more by providing support to other people than it is by receiving support ourselves. The irony of giving is that we get so much more from sharing with others than we do by receiving from them that we're actually both selfish and selfless. A Harvard Business school survey found that regardless of income, people who spent more on others were decidedly happier than those that spent more on themselves. [52] Kabbalistically, the reason we feel unfulfilled is that our own selfish actions have created a barrier between the Creator and us.

To remove this barrier, we need to transform our natures from getting to giving. When you go against your ego, when you share when you least want to, the Light will mimic your actions, making miracles happen in seemingly impossible situations.

Kabbalists teach us that when two people in a relationship treat the other even better than they treat themselves, there is no limit to the amount of blessings they can bring into their lives. Who wouldn't want this? We all do! But it takes discipline to have consistent awareness. It takes doing all those little things, like the check-in call to say, "I understand you're having a hard day. Just know that I'm here for you." Or share with your partner, "I'm really scared. What if my test results indicate that something's wrong?" It takes a conscious coming together because often our exchanges are informed by how we're feeling. We get so immersed in our own experience that we forget that there are two people involved. The key is to have the same depth of empathy for your partner's feelings that you have for your own. This is the prerequisite for the assistance from above: both parties in the relationship must feel selfless love for one another.

There's a kabbalistic parable that expresses this idea. Long ago, a man committed an infraction for which the king condemned him to death. After hearing his sentence, the man turned to the king and asked, "Could I please have a week to put my affairs in order?" The king replied, "I would like to grant you this wish, but I am concerned that you will not return. If you can find somebody who will stay in your place while I set you free for a week, I will let you go. But bear in mind, if you are not back in time to face your sentence, if you are so much as a minute late, I will execute your friend instead."

The condemned man went to his closest friend, whom he had loved since childhood, and asked him, "Can you please do me this favor?" His friend replied, "Of course." The week went by, and the man put his affairs in order. But on his return, he ran into delays on the road. When the hour of his execution came, and he was nowhere to be found, the king decided, "This man has not kept his promise, so I have no choice but to carry out his death sentence on his friend." The royal guards escorted the friend to the gallows to prepare for his hanging.

Just then the man originally sentenced to death ran toward the gallows yelling, "I'm here! I'm here! I was just a little late, but I'm here! I am the one you sentenced to die, so you must set my friend free and put me in his place." But the friend began arguing, "No, the seven days have passed! According to the terms of your agreement, my friend can no longer be put to death. Now I am the one who must be hanged!" Both men pleaded their cases, each begging that he be put to death instead of his friend.

The king, seeing the selfless love between these childhood companions, called for silence. "My original decree called for the death of one man, but I see that the bond between you is so complete that if I carry out that sentence, I will be killing two. Thus, I am forced to rescind my original judgment. You may both go free."

This kind of selfless love is difficult to imagine, let alone attain. I realize this parable sets the bar incredibly high, and my intention is not to make you feel daunted. But it's important to have a goal, and this is what unconditional love looks like. To attain this level of consciousness, it takes years of practice, growth, understanding, and consistently making the choice not to focus on unimportant things. Instead of calculating what your partner has or hasn't done for you, ask yourself, "What have I done for my partner today?" This is the doorway to selfless love.

The Benefits of Being Loved Unconditionally

"The minute I heard my first love story, I started looking for you, not knowing how blind that was. Lovers don't finally meet somewhere; they're in each other all along." — Rumi

The knowledge that we are loved unconditionally creates a safe, secure psychological space. Psychologist Donald Winnicott observed that children playing in close proximity to their mothers display higher levels of creativity than those who were farther away.[53] This "circle of creativity," as he described it, is a space in which children and adults alike can take risks and try things out, fall and stand up again, fail and succeed, because they feel secure in the presence of a person who loves them unconditionally. Adults are capable of higher levels of abstraction than children; we do not need to be physically near our loved ones to be in their circle of creativity. Knowing that we are loved unconditionally makes us feel safe and able to fulfill and manifest our potential. It encourages us to pursue those things that are meaningful to us because sometimes all you need is someone to believe in you when it's too hard to believe in yourself.

My struggle with anorexia was the darkest chapter of my life. I felt alone, lost, and without a clue as to who I was. I was still in the process of healing when Michael and I fell in love. I valued his depth, his spirit, and his truth, even though I couldn't fully embrace mine at the time. But being loved by this amazing soul allowed two things to happen: I learned to love myself as I was, and I discovered I had a huge desire to shed aspects of myself that didn't serve me. That's the power of unconditional love. I was thriving in Michael's circle of creativity. He reassured me, and I, in return, reassured him.

Unconditional love is the nourishment humans need to fulfill their greatness.

A few years ago, I met a couple who had been married for many years. The wife wanted her husband to succeed, but she became frustrated when he couldn't find work, or make headway paying off debts he had accumulated prior to getting married. Eventually, her frustration turned to anger, and the domestic dialogue changed from supportive to denigrating. Oftentimes, she would yell, "You're such a loser." Plus many more expletives. Did she want to use those expletives? Yep! Did she want to call him a loser? Yeah! It felt good at the moment. But she was destroying his circle of creativity.

Of course, she felt badly about her behavior after the fact, but the circle was already broken. If we feel safe knowing that we can try and fail, that we can fall and stand up again, only then are we able to thrive. This is practiced in the best relationships.

Through her harsh words and actions, she, more than anyone else, suffered in the years that followed. Not only did they still have financial worries, but on top of it, they had a broken relationship. To her credit, the wife went to work mending the trust she had broken. She stopped punishing her husband for not doing what she wanted, and instead rededicated herself to the relationship. She still has frustrations from time to time, but she has accepted that for now, she is the primary breadwinner, and she won't allow that to affect her love for him. She encourages her husband to try new things, and she's working very hard to recreate the circle of creativity, a place where he has the opportunity to thrive. This is an example of transformation in action. She is aware that she's not at a place of unconditional love, not yet, but she has an understanding of just how far she has to go, and a strong desire to get there.

A friend of mine pointed out that my husband and I never tell each other what to do. So much so that it's become a joke between us. A typical exchange between us looks something like this:

I'll say, "Honey, I'm so tired. I just don't feel like giving my class tomorrow morning." In the back of my mind, I'm thinking that canceling at the last minute would be irresponsible, which is why I'm deflecting the decision on to him.

He replies, "Sure! Whatever you think."

And we go back and forth like this.

"Really? Can I cancel?"

"Sure, if you're really tired."

He smiles at me during the entire exchange. I know what the right thing to do is, he knows I know, and he knows I'm going to do it. But giving me the freedom to choose makes me feel loved unconditionally, it allows me to be vulnerable, and it reminds me that I'm in a relationship that is supportive, empathetic, and leaves me room to grow as a person and as a wife, while still making his opinion clear.

It's not hard to imagine a way in which the conversation could go quite differently.

"Honey, I'm so tired. I don't feel like giving this class tomorrow morning."

He might reply, "It's really irresponsible of you. You have to give the class."

Or an even more extreme response, "Are you kidding me? Why do you even commit to these things just to cancel them? You are such a flake!"

Based on this dialogue alone, one can see how this will escalate into a fight. In this example, the conversation is riddled with judgment and accusations.

You can redirect the nature of your relationship anytime you decide.

When you love someone else unconditionally, you see the best in them, but you also see the worst, and you love them anyway.

Chapter Fifteen

Soulmates

I was on a secluded beach in Mexico attending the wedding of a close friend, who was sixteen years my senior. The small group of guests was almost all couples in their mid-thirties. Being only twenty-one years old, I felt out of place. The only other person my age was my future husband, Michael, son of the officiating Rabbi. I had met Michael before, just in passing, and being the only two people of a similar age thrown together for a weekend, you'd think we would have naturally gravitated towards each other, but that was not the case.

The day after the wedding, all the guests were outside enjoying the beach. Everywhere I looked there was something exciting happening, parasailers, runners, children making sandcastles, and sunbathers sipping frozen cocktails adorned with tiny umbrellas. As I was taking it all in, enjoying the warmth of the sun on my shoulders, something struck me. I may have felt out of place, but Michael looked out of place. There he sat, uncomfortable and miserable, studying an ancient text in Aramaic, in the heat, desperately trying to cover his entire body, including his head, with a towel. I remember feeling confused. I couldn't figure out why he didn't just go sit in the shade somewhere and put an end to his misery. In hindsight, I realize that he was trying to be part of the group, which didn't come naturally to him.

An avid scholar from a very young age, having fun in the sun was not a priority for Michael, so for him to carry all his books and study in the uneven sand represented a big effort to be social on his part. I can say with absolute certainty that on that day, I did not recognize him as my future husband, let alone my soulmate.

I would love to say that the first time I encountered Michael was life-changing, but in reality, it was more of a thud than a bang. In fact, I'm not

143

even sure you can define our first exchange as a real introduction. We didn't say a single word to each other. The first time I saw him, he was entering a room carrying five books and reading an opened volume on the top of the stack. He looked up as we passed each other and I waved. He nodded in greeting, and then immediately went back to reading. I remember being impressed that he could navigate without bumping into anything while never taking his eyes off the page.

I, on the other hand, spent my time very differently. There was no walking and reading; it was more like drinking and dancing. At 17, attending Beverly Hills High School, I was a free spirit. I drove my Jeep Wrangler around town, my long curly hair blowing in the wind. I lived in Levi's and motorcycle boots. Michael was 18 at the time, and he didn't just read books, he inhaled them. He didn't put much importance on superficial things, so wearing black pants and a white shirt every day suited him just fine.

The differences between Michael and me were obvious, from how we dressed, to how we spent our time, to how we grew up (he was born in Jerusalem and lived an Orthodox Jewish life, where I was born in Louisiana and, although raised Jewish, sang a lot of Christmas carols growing up). That day on the beach in Mexico, I was relying solely on my five senses. From my perspective in the 1%, I couldn't see that we had anything in common at all.

Soulmates Are Not Who We Think They Are

As I can tell you from firsthand experience, you may not recognize your soulmate at first, and finding that person has absolutely nothing to do with how you look, your status, or how often you date. Most of us limit the experience of true love to affection, mental stimulation, physical desire, and chemistry. A soulmate isn't necessarily someone that you have the greatest chemistry with, that you look great with in pictures, that you have overwhelmingly passionate feelings for or even the person you have the greatest sex with. This is not to say you *won't* have those things, but soulmate love is not based on the five senses.

According to Kabbalah, in the beginning, all souls were one, and the Creator split each soul into two parts, male and female. And when I say male and female, I'm not talking about physical anatomy or gender. I am referring to the two basic energies in the Universe: the desire to impart (masculine energy) and the desire to receive (feminine energy). Soulmates are those two halves of a single soul. This means that each one of us has a male or female complement in this world. However, soulmates may go many lifetimes without reuniting, marrying others in the meantime, with whom they may create loving and satisfying lives. These connections are no less valid, as Kabbalah teaches that everyone that enters our life is a part of *shoresh* (root of the soul). Rav Isaac Luria, also known as the Ari, explains that if you look at all of humanity as a tree, two souls that come from the same branch are connected. Anyone in your life–whether it's a friend, a lover, or a business partner–you experience a closeness with those people because you are from the same root of the soul.

Having the same root of the soul brings with it a responsibility, regardless of the nature of the relationship. I have an obligation to assist these people I'm connected to, not just physically, but also spiritually. No meeting in our lives is coincidental, therefore no one who comes into our close circle does so by accident. They all have a reason for being in our lives and are part of our tikkune. Part of our spiritual process is to understand the ways in which we are responsible for helping the people with whom we share a *shoresh* (root of the soul).

KABBALISTIC PRINCIPLE:

Kabbalah teaches that one obtains a mate according to their deeds and behavior.

· · · · · · · ·

Reuniting two separate halves of the same soul takes hard work. We have to earn and deserve the reunification with our soulmate through our spiritual journey and process. I often ask my students this question: What is the one thing you leave this world with? The answer is your soul. If transformation were at the forefront of your thoughts, then where you place your effort would look quite different. The more energy you put into your transformation correlates to how quickly you and your soulmate are reunited. This can take more than one lifetime, but when two souls have worked hard enough on their spiritual paths and on correcting their tikkune, they merit coming together. The two halves become one.

Michael and I are an example of the unexpected nature of soulmate reunions. In the years following the day we met at the wedding, I became very involved in studying and volunteering at The Kabbalah Centre where Michael was not only a Kabbalah scholar, but also the son of the Centre's co-directors. We had a handful of brief exchanges, which were initiated by Michael, which was unusual because he was not one for small talk. On one of his visits to Los Angeles, after not having seen him for over six months, he was suddenly in front of me asking how I was 'doing these days.' I began telling him that I was interested in Psychology as a major and Marine Biology as a minor, but before I could even finish the sentence, he just walked away. I had no idea what to make of it (was he being deliberately rude, or was he just clueless?), but it started me thinking.

The truth of the matter was that on some level, I wasn't comfortable pursuing my course of study because I wanted to become a serious student of Kabbalah. After my bruised ego was assuaged, I understood why it bothered me: He was aware of something I hadn't quite come to terms with.

Those are the signs. This person that I'd spoken ten words to knew my future, one that I didn't yet have access to. He hadn't walked away abruptly because he was rude or uninterested; there was something deeper behind his actions. He recognized the potential in my spiritual development before I did, and he was uncomfortable even to hear about distractions that might take me down a different, less authentic path.

I respected how seriously Michael took his studies and the discipline he applied. I also felt his behavior was too extreme and didn't leave

146

enough room for friendships or outside interests. Neither of us was sure what to make of these exchanges. I've come to understand that there are moments in life that may seem insignificant at the time that turn out to be monumental in hindsight. I had several of these seemingly innocuous moments with Michael that later turned out to be significant. We didn't have long conversations, Michael rarely entered into dialogue with anyone, so the fact that he spoke to me at all meant something. We just didn't know what, at that point.

Three years after that day on the beach, Michael was working on an important project, and he needed creative input. He asked a mutual friend to approach me about working on the project with him. At that point, I was enrolled in college, working part-time as a teacher, and volunteering in my spare time. Overwhelmed by these commitments, I turned down the request three times. Unwilling to disappoint Michael, our mutual friend wouldn't take no for an answer, though, and finally, I acquiesced.

Weeks later, when I walked into Michael's office to present what I had worked on, I felt a little bit nervous. As I laid my papers out on his desk, our hands touched, and I remember feeling and seeing sparks. Like Xanadu! Michael tells the story this way. "One second, she was in my office, and we were talking, and then something – I would say divine – happened. It was almost like the creation of the world; the moment before there was nothing and the moment after there was everything. Nine months later, we were married. It's a long and short love story."

There were so many things about us that didn't seem to match up, yet Michael and I had no doubts, no second thoughts, not one moment of hesitation from that moment our hands first touched. In the months that followed, we discovered the unseen ways we did match. Whereas on the outside we were unlikely, on the inside nothing else could have made more sense.

We were young. I was 23, and Michael was 24 when we got married. Neither of us had been in a relationship with anyone before; between the two of us, we had a total of zero relationship experience. Yet we had so much fun working and playing together that we never wanted to be apart again. I don't remember ever laughing as hard as I did with Michael in those early days. The overarching feeling was one of simply being understood. It felt rare.

We instinctively entrusted ourselves to each other in a way we had never done with anyone else before.

"A sign of love is something so subtle, it's just there. It's an overwhelming feeling of not wanting to be apart from this person for one moment."
— Rav Berg [54]

Things take time before their potential can be revealed. Those brief exchanges that I didn't understand at the time were really an indication that we were on similar paths until the day our paths converged. To be able to recognize Michael as my life's partner, I needed to view people and situations from a spiritual place rather than merely from a place of limitation (ruled by the five senses). As your consciousness elevates, you gain a greater understanding of how the world works. You begin operating with a deeper sense of what's real and what's not. When you navigate life from this conscious place, the information that you're getting isn't coming from what you see, hear, or feel, but it comes from deep within. Consciousness is evolution, and the more evolved you become, the more capable you are of recognizing your soulmate.

Kabbalah's teachings on soulmates are explored at length in the Zohar. This timeless wisdom describes what we must do to bring our soulmates into our lives. It is written in the portion of the Zohar called Lech Lecha, verse 348: "We have learned that a man obtains a mate according to his deeds and ways of his behavior. If he is meritorious and his ways are correct, then he deserves his soulmate, to join her as they were before coming down to this world."

Many people I counsel beg for the answer to their most important life's question, "How do I find my soulmate?" and air grievances such as, "I'm not sure the guy I'm dating is my soulmate because...." The danger of obsessing over finding a soulmate relationship is that one can become overly focused on the idea of finding their soulmate rather than finding a life partner that is fun, loving, nurturing and who they can grow with. In reality, very few do find their true soulmates, but anyone can have a relationship that consists of all the things a soulmate relationship does.

148

To be clear, it's less important to be certain that you're with your soulmate than it is to treat every relationship with a soulmate-level of respect, where appreciation and unconditional love are expressed daily.

An example of this can be found in a couple I have counseled for many years. Both people are lovely and have healthy relationships with friends and family. They share a nice lifestyle, have two sweet children, and things are much improved from where they were when we started working together many years ago. Gone are the screaming matches and physical altercations, as both husband and wife have learned healthier, more respectful ways of communicating. What I've come to understand, however, is that no matter how much counseling I provide, no matter how many tools I share with them, or how much improvement they have made, they are not a source of joy for one another. Why? Because on some level they have decided that they are not soulmates and there is a more viable partner waiting to be discovered. If I could guarantee that they had married their soulmate, they'd actually give their marriage a fighting chance.

Most people understand a soulmate relationship as one in which they will feel elated; the relationship will feel effortless and mirror something close to perfection. Like most people, Michael and I assumed that being in love was the way to fulfill all our desires and needs—a way to receive everything we needed and wanted. However, this is not the basis for a loving relationship. Part of the problem here is one of the definitions. We might say that we love eating pizza or that we love going to baseball games, but "love" in this context is just a word that describes a pleasurable sensation. It's comprised entirely of our own experience, without any giving on our part. This is perfectly reasonable with regard to food or entertainment, but love is much more than enjoying another person. A soulmate is someone who aids you to transform from a life based on getting to one based on giving. That's a big transformation.

Ethan was married to a very kind, loving, and amenable woman. Each day after work she would greet him at the door with a Highland Park Scotch (neat) in one hand, take his briefcase with the other, and follow him up the stairs to the bathroom where the bath she had drawn was waiting. While he soaked, she'd pull up a stool and rub his back with a washcloth, only interjecting to offer words of encouragement and love, while she listened to him talk all about his day. Naturally, the children were already bathed and doing homework, and the table was set for the family to eat dinner when Ethan was ready.

Ethan had a very nice, comfortable life with his wife. She didn't challenge, question, or provoke him. She loved him dearly and went out of her way to accommodate his desires. Most people are searching for this very thing, but in truth, it doesn't lead to a satisfying life. In fact, it breeds boredom. Time and time again, I meet men and women whose biggest complaint is that they don't have anything in common with their partner anymore; they're evolving separately rather than together. As a result, they don't have much to talk about other than the children or which restaurant they are going to choose for dinner. They don't feel stimulated mentally; therefore, don't feel emotionally connected. Instead of looking for fun things to do together, they're often looking for distractions outside of the relationship to assuage their boredom. Naturally, the ebbs and flows of life guarantee that we'll feel bored from time to time, but when you find yourself feeling uninspired by your relationship, it's time to inject your relationship with something new.

"Boredom comes from unmet or abandoned potential." — Michael Berg [55]

As it turned out, Ethan was deeply unhappy in this relationship, despite his wife's best efforts. Although he had sought comfort and ease from his marriage, he came to understand that what he really wanted was to be challenged, questioned and provoked in a way that would inspire him, pique his curiosity, and lead to new ways of thinking and being. He wanted a person to share this journey with him. He made the painful decision to break up his family, and it was especially difficult because, after all, she was fulfilling the relationship expectations that he had set.

The irony here is that Ethan and his wife would have been better off with more discomfort in their relationship. Boredom is a sure sign that you are in a rut, not pushing yourself to experience something new—and the discomfort that comes along with it. Kabbalists have long known that discomfort is the ejection seat to elevated consciousness, and to greater enjoyment of life.

We tend to think that our relationship is difficult because we married the wrong person, but every marriage has its nagging problems that require attention. A person might say about their partner, "I never felt this frustrated with anyone before. Only my spouse makes me feel this way, and he brings out the absolute worst in me, so it must be his fault." But actually, the opposite is true. Rather than dealing with the issues in that relationship, people instead either fantasize about or look for a new relationship with someone who won't challenge them and with whom they can experience a feel-good, easy exchange.

When couples have seemingly irreconcilable differences or nasty fights, these negative times actually have the greatest potential to create intimacy. The key word here is potential. While difficult, these are opportunities for growth and transformation in your relationship and have the power to elevate love.

The foundation of Kabbalah is change. We speak about change, we learn about it, we try it, and yet there is nothing of a physical or spiritual nature in this world more difficult than changing.

When we think of change, we're usually considering making modifications within our comfort zone, not taking into consideration how incredibly difficult real change is. A soulmate relationship will thrust you outside that comfort zone, which, ultimately, may not be something you genuinely want. In order to enter into a soulmate relationship, you can't avoid the pain that is inextricably intertwined with change. No real change can happen without disruption, flexibility, and pain! It requires a major shift in who you are, which means you have to be malleable and willing to stretch.

As I mentioned, I had to change and grow in order to see Michael as my life partner. By nature, I'm a very organized person. I like schedules and routines and find great comfort in them. I wasn't fully aware how much my life would change once we were married, nor did I appreciate how attached I was to the security of my routine until I had to change it. It took time to embrace the idea that part of my life's work with Michael required travel. When I was growing up, my family traveled maybe once a year. Consistent travel was very outside of my comfort zone. But, instead of fighting that change, I shifted my mindset so I could see what a gift it is to wake up in a different city and have experiences that could never be planned. Today there is a suitcase by the door pretty much all the time.

If Michael were left to his own devices, he'd be perfectly happy to sit alone in a room and study all day. For the first few years of our marriage, the majority of his time was spent in quiet study while I was more comfortable speaking and connecting with people. We both had the potential to influence people in many different ways, yet we were limited in only putting energy into what came easily for us. What came easily to him was more difficult for me and vice versa. This is the most profound way in which we have influenced each other throughout our marriage. I'm not sure without each other's "uncomfortable pushing" that we could have revealed our untapped potential.

Michael, for example, is a powerful speaker and teacher. As for me, quiet study and learning have become an integral part of my life that I would never have imagined would be such a source of growth and happiness for me. This process of change wasn't easy or natural for either one of us. But once we were open to each other's encouragement and began to change, we would not go back to our old ways for anything. Eventually, we came to enjoy that which we thought we never would. Relationships should be fulfilling, but a couple's greater purpose is to push each other in ways that are uncomfortable. The success of our marriage is based on the fact that Michael and I don't necessarily make life easier for each other, but we do constantly bend, and we challenge, push, and change each other for the better.

How to Bend

Let's look at the very nature of a relationship. It starts with two unique individuals who come together to cohabitate, love, and hopefully grow, all while blending their backgrounds, personal tastes, families, incomes, sex drives, careers, and friends. It's a miracle that people can actually cohabitate! In relationships, when couples are inflexible, they experience greater levels of unhappiness and disappointments, which lead to more frequent arguments.

To transform judgment, frustration, and rage into more elevated emotions, like empathy, kindness, and love, you have to be flexible. Practically, here are a few examples to help you bend.

Realize, This Too Shall Pass

A couple moved to a new city where the wife was struggling with feelings of not fully belonging. She was taking it out on her husband, because he made friends more easily, and he had initiated this move. The advice I gave her was, "This too shall pass." There are people out there waiting for you to be their friend. You'll make new friends. It takes time. You can't just move and have everything already be in place. And most importantly, remember that new friends are fun to make. You are likable. Know that you are not alone in how you feel; everyone is the new kid at some point. Instead of blaming your husband realize that you have a friend in him first and foremost, and work toward building a life together in this new city.

Some Things Just Are What They Are

If you have asked your partner to put their dirty clothes directly into the hamper once a day for the past six years, instead of blaming your mother-in-law for not raising your partner right, it may be time to accept that your reality is one that usually has dirty clothes spread on the floor. Or you can come up with a creative solution.

I'm a very neat person and Michael, not so much. When we were first married, imagine my shock to find trails of clothing everywhere. I did not know this about him! After three years of nagging him to hang up his clothes and tiring of hearing my own voice, I decided that instead of getting frustrated that no progress had been made I took a moment to see the reasons why he was seemingly so inflexible and why his inability to hang up his clothes bothered me so much. I realized about myself that when I see dirt or clutter, it affects my mood. Michael, on the other hand, could wear crumpled, wrinkled shirts all week and he'd still be chipper. It wasn't that he was intentionally not taking my request seriously — disorder just doesn't affect him.

I got him a chair that sat in the corner of our bedroom where he could pile his clothes all week, and come Friday he'd hang them up. That was a compromise that worked for both of us. If you use this approach, you are now free to spend your energy and time thinking about more important things than improperly discarded clothing.

How Important is it, Really?

Most of the time, the things that have our hearts racing and blood boiling are quite inconsequential. Like, clothes or, for that matter, toast.

Jacob and Michelle are otherwise very sane, kind people, who both became unutterably enraged at each other over the proper level of toastedness that a piece of bread should be to give to a teething toddler. There were tears, recriminations. Even the next day, there were attempts to validate the rightness of their assertions as to the appropriate level of toastedness. Obviously, there were underlying issues that fed the toast conflict. When you find yourself getting heated over something ridiculous, take a breath. Simply identifying that you are having a 'toast' moment is all it takes to restore levity and calm. Now, if there is an underlying issue, be flexible and decide to repair the hiccup in the relationship instead of damaging it further.

Chapter Sixteen

Mirror, Mirror on the Wall

It's not uncommon for people in relationships to want their partner to improve in ways that match up with their own ideals. But who we think our partner should be often turns out to have little basis in reality. It only ends up limiting who they can become. There is no such thing as an ideal person, but with the insight provided by the mirror you and your partner hold up to each other, you can help each other evolve. The problem is that when people don't like what they see, they blame the mirror.

Rav Ashlag teaches that we can't give a name to anything we can't imagine. When we look at who we are and where we want to be, it's limited because it is all within the framework of what we know. This is where our partner can help us if they can set aside their own idea of who we should be and see us in terms of our potential. Think of it this way: If you've been blind all your life, a new technological breakthrough may make it possible for you to have an operation that suddenly allows you to see. Once the bandages are removed, technically you're no longer blind, but it will take you quite some time to understand what it is you're looking at. Our potential works much the same way. We need new situations and new people to reveal that hidden and unrevealed potential we possess. This is the importance of having a help-mate and a life partner—to show us these situations, to help us manifest our potential, and in turn, to help them manifest theirs.

Research supports this idea that we can help shape our partners into better versions of themselves. Professor Stephen Michael Drigotas at Johns Hopkins University coined the phrase the "Michelangelo Phenomenon" to describe the process by which partners gently sculpt each other into a more desirable version of the self. [56] Michelangelo Phenomenon is the idea that we all have a better version of ourselves waiting to be revealed through assistance from another person. Sociologist Charles Horton Cooley referred to the phenomenon as the "looking glass self."

To illustrate this phenomenon, let's take a look at Daniel and Jasmine. Daniel was always plagued by caring too much about what people thought and, being an introvert, all of this self-doubt made him a wallflower. Then he met Jasmine. She laughed at his jokes, set up his one-liners at parties, and always encouraged him to be himself. With Jasmine cheering him on, Daniel became more confident. Soon he became the life of the party and gained the confidence he had lacked most of his life.

The point here isn't to fix what you perceive as your partner's flaws. The Michelangelo Phenomenon only works if your ideal image of your partner is aligned with his ideal image. In the case of Jasmine and Daniel, she helped him uncover qualities he'd always wanted to access. He may have been introverted with other people, but not with Jasmine. She loved the person she saw in him, helped him share that special person with others, and in the process shifted his image of himself.

On the contrary, if a man wanted to sculpt his wife into Marilyn Monroe when she aspires to be more like Joan of Arc, it's undoubtedly going to cause dissonance. Not because either image is better or worse, but because they are at odds. One is true to her, and the other is who he wants her to be. To benefit from the Michelangelo Phenomenon, we need to be committed to becoming our authentic self, versus someone else's version of who we should be.

"I've had at least three marriages. They've just all been with the same person." — Ada Calhoun [57]

Not surprisingly, there's also a dark side to this ability to influence each other. Partners can propel each other either closer to or farther away from their ideal vision of self. When a partner acts in ways that limit your potential by trying to impose their ideas of what you should be, this is known as the Golem Effect, [58] which is the opposite of the Michelangelo Phenomenon. The Golem Effect illustrates how one's performance suffers when someone places low expectations upon them. Just as we can support and gently shape our partners in a positive way, we also have the power to discourage our partners by putting too much focus on what they aren't doing, how they aren't being, and what they aren't giving.

Do you encourage your partner to grow in positive ways? Or are you quick to point out where he or she falls short? Do you label your partner as withholding, inconsiderate, judgmental, or cold?

I can't stress how important it is not to label those we love. By not assigning them as any one thing, we allow them to be so many things.

Michelangelo has said of his creations, such as his sculptures of David and Moses, that they were already inside the blocks of marble before he started sculpting them. In the best relationships, not only are you thinking about who you want to be, but your partner is as well. They are willing to help you get there by becoming your ally in sculpting your ideal self and bringing out the person you dream of becoming. This process can lead to personal growth and long-term satisfaction both in life and the relationship. An ideal partner supports your dreams, traits, and the qualities that you want to develop, whether you've fully articulated them or not.

I've always had the same motivation for the work I do. It's always been about elevating consciousness and empowering myself and others to live happy and fulfilling lives. While my motivation didn't change, the way I wanted to express it did. Before my desire changed, I sat behind a desk, doing important work, but not connecting to people in a real, intimate way, a way that I truly craved and knew in my heart would be of greater benefit to myself and the world. I no longer felt inspired or satisfied. I didn't feel that it was what I was supposed to be doing anymore. So for a year I struggled with how to move forward.

Over the years, I shared with Michael my growing desire to speak in public, to write, and to serve as a mentor. Or 'Having such a desire was intimidating.' I had a fear of failure, and a 'better the devil you know than the one you don't' mentality. I kept wavering. Should I do it? And Michael said to me, "You know what, Monica? A lot of people in this world would rather you just sit behind that desk for the rest of your life, and they'd be totally fine with you doing that. But if you feel this is what you need to do, then go and do it. I believe in you. It's time you start believing in yourself."

Michael's words provided me with a major aha-moment because what he had said was true and simple, yet profound. Whether I would fail or succeed, I needed to try. It took him believing in me enough for both of us and, through his words, I felt like he was starting to chisel away at my unmet potential.

KABBALISTIC PRINCIPLE:

On a spiritual level, energy comes to this world without form; the way we think about things and the way we speak about them makes that form manifest.

· · · · · · · ·

If couples often judge their partners and have thoughts such as "They have such a bad attitude," "I can't believe he/she made that choice again," "That is so wrong"—then they have brought an equal amount of darkness into their life. This is a powerful teaching, but it doesn't need to incite fear or dread. It can be an incredible tool for self-awareness. Everyone has good and bad; duality is a necessary part of our lives, but choose to focus on the good and encourage your partner's growth.

Chapter Seventeen

What Are You Saying?

"Keep your tongue from evil and your lips from speaking negatively. Refrain from evil and do good, seek peace, and pursue it." — Psalms 34:13-15

. . . .

The kabbalists teach that when we leave this world, all the things that we have said are repeated back to us. Take a moment to let that sink in: Every single word you've uttered is repeated back. Upon this recitation, and probably with great shock, we finally understand the power of our words. Unfortunately, we will only come to a complete appreciation of the power of speech after we leave this world.

Even the most innocuous phrases can cause damage. I feel like I am forever correcting my friends when they say things like "I could have died it was so embarrassing," or "This is killing me." This kind of speech, even though it seems innocent, could not be more pernicious. This is the way most people speak without ever noticing it.

- "She's completely self-involved."
- "I'm so angry at him. I could just strangle him!"
- "They just bought a new car, but are three months behind on their light bill!"
- "Can you believe the way she treats her step-daughter?"

If you're human, those little phrases probably piqued your interest. "Tell me more!" screams everything in your psyche. It's normal. Most of the time, our lives are dominated by external influences. By someone or something that upsets us, a political event, a sideways remark from a co-worker, or an action taken seemingly against us by a friend or family member. How

159

many times have you reached out to a friend expressing the need to vent about something that is bothering you? Pretty often, I'm sure. While this isn't inherently bad—communicating our feelings in a conscious way is actually a very good thing—if we aren't careful, we'll end up slipping from venting a frustration to gossiping.

Merriam Webster defines gossip as "a person who habitually reveals personal or sensational facts about others" and a "rumor or report of an intimate nature."

Evil speech, or what kabbalists refer to as Lashon Hara, meaning "evil tongue" in Hebrew, is the worst form of darkness. Lashon Hara is understood with this story of a shopkeeper who lived in a small village. He was a pleasant man, but he had a disagreeable habit of gossiping. He enjoyed all the attention he got from people stopping by his shop to hear the latest rumors. He knew what he was doing was wrong, but he couldn't help himself. One day, he heard the most outrageous story about another man in the village. He knew that if this story got around, it would damage the man's reputation, but the tale was so juicy that he couldn't resist, so he told a few people.

Hearing the awful rumor circulating about him, the man went to the town's mayor in despair. "What am I to do?" he wailed. "If people believe this about me, I'll be ruined!"

The mayor, knowing who had spread the rumor, spoke to the shopkeeper. The shopkeeper felt badly that the man was so upset, but after all, he hadn't been the one who started the rumor, and honestly, how bad could it be just to repeat a story? The mayor sighed and asked the shopkeeper if he had a feather pillow and then instructed him to take the pillow outside and cut it open.

"But that will make a mess!" the shopkeeper protested. But the mayor insisted, and the shopkeeper finally cut open the pillow. There happened to be a stiff breeze sweeping through the town that day, so all the feathers burst out of the pillowcase in a swirling cloud and flew into the air. Some flew into people's windows, others landed in trees, and still others were scattered across the nearby farmers' fields.

"Now put all the feathers back in the pillowcase," instructed the mayor.

"But I can't!" protested the shopkeeper. "By now they're scattered all across town. Some of them are surely gone forever!" "Exactly. Once a word leaves your mouth, it flies on the wings of the wind, and you can never get it back."

Once people have heard gossip, the words have changed them. They have new perceptions based on the gossip, and those new perceptions can't easily be erased.

This story clearly illustrates the universal truth: once a negative word is said, it's said. Once people have heard gossip, the words have changed them. They have new perceptions based on the gossip, and those new perceptions can't easily be erased. Next time you're enticed to share a juicy story or be the recipient of one, run it through Socrates' triple filter test.

Onc day, one of Socrates students approached him and excitedly shared, "Socrates, I have just heard some news about one of your friends."

"Before you tell me this news, we need to make sure that it passes through the triple filter test," responded Socrates.

"What is that?" asked his student.

"The first test is truth. Do you know what you're about to tell me is absolutely true?" asked Socrates. The man thought, and then responded, "I heard it from someone else, so I'm not sure if it's all true."

"The second filter is goodness. Is what you have to tell me something good?" Socrates queried.

"No, it's not good," his student responded.

"So, what you have to tell me is neither true nor good," Socrates replied.

The man was embarrassed. Socrates continued, the third and final filter is usefulness. Is what you have to share useful?"

"Probably not," the man replied.

"If you are not going to tell me something true, good, or useful, then why tell me at all?"

Evil speech is more than just speaking negatively about someone else; it also includes those times when we speak in anger, and when we talk about ourselves in a disparaging way. Just as gossiping, and saying angry or negative things to others is dangerous, so too is sitting around and talking about how bad things are or how bad they will become.

KABBALISTIC PRINCIPLE:

Every deed we perform, each emotion we display, and every word we speak is reflected back to our lives in equal measure, and in identical tone, by the universe.

········

There is a couple who love each other very much, but when they fight the wife will routinely say, "I want a divorce!" Every single time. She knows she shouldn't utter those words, but she can't control herself. Afterward, she always feels horrible, and understandably so. After we had lengthy discussions, she came to appreciate just how much she was affected by the bitter divorce of her parents, which took ten years to settle. Every argument with her husband transports her back to her childhood, where all roads eventually lead to one painful outcome: divorce.

"Speak when you're angry, and you will make the best speech you will ever regret." — Groucho Marx [59]

No matter how strong our reasons may be, some things should never be said. Rav Berg put it this way: "It can take two seconds to destroy something that took years to build." Such is the power of words.

162

Imagine that you are planting an orchard, and that orchard is your life. You can plant seeds for apple trees, or olive trees, whatever you fancy, but the all-important decision must be made just before you plant the seed.

Once you've planted it, the die is cast. The same is true for words: when you're still forming them in your mind, you can make them come out any way you choose. But once they're uttered, there's no going back. In potential, you can change anything. Once it is manifested, however, you cannot. An apple tree cannot grow olives, just as a negative word cannot create positive outcomes. This is why it's so important to watch what you say and to refrain from evil speech as much as possible. Especially in romantic relationships, the oneness and intimacy that you share can be shattered by ill-spoken words. It is for this reason that during a kabbalistic wedding a glass is shattered by the groom. The glass represents the marriage, reminding us to be gentle with each other lest we do irreparable harm to the relationship. Here we acknowledge that there will be times during the marriage when we may damage the relationship through our actions or words. When a glass is broken and shattered into millions of pieces, it can never be put back together quite the same again.

With mindfulness, we can begin to shift our consciousness toward seeing the good in others (and ourselves), which will naturally change the way we speak.

If you want to know who a person is you have to listen to what comes out of their mouth, or more importantly, what are the things that they espouse as being important. What are the ideas that they elevate?

The conversations we have hold clues and indications of our state of consciousness. For instance, a person who in conversation exalts acts of kindness, a commitment to growth, and generosity values the same. If negative thoughts are in your mind, inevitably negative words will leave your mouth.

David Foster Wallace, spoke eloquently to this idea in a commencement speech he gave:

"In the day-to-day trenches of adult life, there is actually no such thing as atheism. There is no such thing as not worshipping. Everybody worships. The only choice we get is what to worship. And an outstanding reason for choosing some sort of God or spiritual-type thing to worship—be it J.C. or Allah, be it Yahweh or the Wiccan mother-goddess or the Four Noble Truths or some infrangible set of ethical principles—is that pretty much anything else you worship will eat you alive. If you worship money and things—if they are where you tap real meaning in life—then you will never have enough. Never feel you have enough. It's the truth. Worship your own body and beauty and sexual allure, and you will always feel ugly, and when time and age start showing, you will die a million deaths before they finally plant you. On one level, we all know this stuff already—it's been codified as myths, proverbs, clichés, bromides, epigrams, parables: the skeleton of every great story. The trick is keeping the truth up-front in daily consciousness. Worship power—you will feel weak and afraid, and you will need ever more power over others to keep the fear at bay. Worship your intellect, being seen as smart—you will end up feeling stupid, a fraud, always on the verge of being found out."

What we worship, what we exalt, becomes our life, both in our thoughts and our words. The question is not whether you are perfect or are doing only positive actions and not negative actions. The question is, what is the most exalted thing in your mind?

If the most exalted thing in your mind is your connection to the Creator, then you are connected to your source.

There is a parable of a spiritual teacher who was walking with his students when they came upon the body of a dead cow in an advanced state of decomposition. The students said to their teacher: "That cow smells terrible!" The teacher replied: "You know, I am not sure about the smell, but look how white the cow's teeth are."

And somehow the way he said it, his students started feeling bad about commenting on the smell of that dead animal. They understood that if it is bad to speak negatively about a dead, decomposing cow, so much more so is it not right to speak negatively about a person.

If it is good to find something good about the decaying carcass of a dead cow, how much more important it is to find the goodness in people and speak about that. It is possible to find good in even the most distressing situation, see the white teeth in the dead decaying cow. Perhaps the great teacher did smell the carcass, but he was not consciously connecting to that. He knew if he wanted to connect to the Light, he needed to look for the good.

You only have two choices of what you connect to in this life. You can connect to the state of goodness—which means seeing what is good about yourself, someone else, or your circumstances.

Or you can connect to everything that is wrong, and there is ALWAYS something you can find.

Before you do speak, think about the effect your words will have.

If your words don't support what you intend to put out in the world, don't say them.

Chapter Eighteen

Spiritual Sparring

Whenever we react without thinking, we're already on treacherous ground. One of the basic principles of Kabbalah is that when we react to any person, whether it be in anger or any other negative emotion, we become the effect of our life, and not the cause. What do I mean by this? There are two kinds of behavior: proactive and reactive.

KABBALISTIC PRINCIPLE:

When challenges occur in our lives, we can choose to have a proactive or reactive consciousness.

. . . .

When you are proactive, you are actively shaping your life the way you want it to be; you're the cause. Proactive consciousness results in momentary discomfort but long-term fulfillment. Conversely, when you are reactive, you're responding to whatever comes up, so you're the effect; you're giving up your power. Reactive consciousness results in thought, words, and deeds that create instant gratification but long-term chaos. Reactive behavior is an ego-based response to something that upsets you without taking a moment to consider the bigger picture or the other person's perspective. This is what creates most of the arguments between couples.

This is where the kabbalistic tool of restriction comes in. Restriction is the practice of remaining non-reactive in a challenging situation—to not lash out in anger, or not speak unkindly when confronted with adverse behavior or circumstances.

167

The Proactive Formula

Step 1: Pause before you react. When an obstacle or challenge arises, remember that your reaction—not the problem—is the real issue. Events in our lives are inherently neutral. They only become "good" or "bad" once we react to them. Pay attention to what sets you off to help you avoid those triggers. Identify why you're feeling angry or reactive.

Think back to a time when you lost your temper. Did you stop to examine why you were frustrated or did you just act on it? Earlier, I discussed feeling your emotions but not becoming the emotion. The proactive formula is the perfect tool to use to navigate your emotions. Remembering to bring this logical awareness to moments when you are triggered, even mildly, will help you mitigate your reactivity.

Step 2: Apply Restriction. Once you have identified a trigger when it arises, take a moment before responding. Ask the Light for help in finding the best proactive solution. In moments of tension, seek out a response that will promote peace. If you do react, take a few deep breaths and remind yourself that anger and judgment only create separation and chaos. Your increased awareness of restriction as a tool will go a long way toward creating unity in your relationship.

The concept of restriction is a bit tricky because it's easily confused with repression. Repression involves ignoring or pushing aside your true thoughts and feelings. It creates just as much turmoil as reactivity.

Step 3: Take proactive action. Understand that the situation at hand is an opportunity for you. If you're unsure which choice is reactive and which proactive, the quickest path to clarity is to ask yourself which option requires the greater stretch. Proactive choices in relationships aren't usually comfortable or gratifying, but they create trust and closeness. Reactive choices (like venting your anger with a hostile diatribe) provide instant gratification, but ultimately create greater complications. Choose the response that asks you to be the bigger person, even if it requires more of you than you think you can provide at that moment.

As we know, anger is one of the primary reactive responses, and it tends to be the biggest challenge for couples. Anger is our reaction when we feel offended, wronged, or denied and often fuels an instant desire for retaliation. Learning an alternative response, in this case, a way to use your anger as a tool for growth, provides an enormous benefit.

"Anger is like drinking poison and expecting the other to die." — Buddha

The Physiology of Anger

We have considered anger a few times now, but we haven't yet looked at how anger manifests for men and women physiologically. You may be surprised to learn that in some ways, it's different. However, we all share a process in which our heart rate increases, preparing us to move, blood flows to our hands, preparing them to strike, our blood pressure elevates, and our adrenaline levels rise. Researchers have done studies on the physiological effects of arguing and the measurable changes that occur in our bodies when we fight.

When we think about things that hurt us, even when they are not happening or in our presence, our body still reacts as if it is in danger. It activates what is known as the fight or flight response. The body releases stress hormones to prepare us to respond to danger either through fighting back or running away, while the liver dumps cholesterol into our bloodstream so that we will clot more easily in case we lose blood.

When we're having an argument or disagreement, men and women typically process their emotions differently. Women find it difficult to separate their personal experiences from problems, while men tend to separate or remove their personal connection from the problem. Men also tend to be able to focus, or do, only one thing at a time, unlike women who have the capacity to focus on multiple things at once, taking a broad view of a problem and considering solutions in terms of their interconnectedness.

When disagreeing with your partner, remember that men tend to consider problems one piece at a time. In fact, they are prone to minimizing details that may be crucial to achieving a solution. And unlike a woman, a man may repeatedly work through the same problem—even talking about the same thing again and again—instead of addressing the problem all at once like women tend to do.

In a typical argument, women make demands and men, in response, shut down and withdraw, which in turn infuriates women! This demand-withdrawal dynamic is a classic pattern that I think we've all experienced. But here's the very illuminating thing—each response has striking corollaries within the body. There is something physiological happening when a man shuts down. He finds it calming to withdraw from conflict; his heart rate drops, and his breathing slows as he pulls away. Even for the alpha male who never backs away from a fight, it comes down to stamina, and eventually, all men retreat to maintain their equilibrium.

Women, on the other hand, respond to their partner's withdrawal with growing frustration, wondering, "Why won't he talk to me?" Her heart rate raises, and her breathing becomes shallow and short. The more he withdraws, the more physiologically aroused she becomes. The body is fundamentally involved in the relationship, but few of us pay attention to it. Men are more easily overwhelmed by marital conflict than their wives. Perhaps you wouldn't think so, but it's true. Men take longer to recover from loud noises than women. This is because the male cardiovascular system remains more reactive than the female's, and is slower to recover from stress.

Understanding this allows us to have empathy for each other. For women, this withdrawal behavior that makes us nuts is very calming for him. He cannot respond in any other way, so let him withdraw, but make sure you tell him to come back in 10 minutes. And men, know that when you withdraw, it will naturally trigger women. No one can read minds, so simply express, "I need 5 or 10 minutes, and then we can talk about it." That's it. It's that simple. Men are not shutting down because they don't value what their partner has to say or because they want to upset them—they just respond to the stress differently. Conversely, women don't want to nag or berate, which is why being able to step back and say, "Okay, I'll give you the time," can be an equally simple shift that creates big rewards.

Three Types of Anger

Psychologists have broken down anger into three different types. The first is **hasty and sudden** anger and is connected to our impulse for self-preservation. It is similar to the primal response animals exhibit when they feel threatened. It can occur when we feel tormented or trapped when we are in physical danger, or for instance, when we're cut off on the freeway. Like animals, when we experience sudden anger, we make loud sounds in an attempt to look larger and more intimidating. We glare as a warning to aggressors to stop their threatening behavior. When people persist in this type of anger, they do things they would not otherwise do.

How many times have we been told by somebody after they flew into a rage, "I'm so sorry. I don't know what came over me. That's so unlike me." The story of Tiger Woods comes to mind. When his wife found out that he was cheating, she took his golf clubs to his car, but she wasn't helping to put them in the trunk; she used them to shatter all the windows! [61] Ordinarily, she probably wouldn't have dreamed of doing that, but in the throes of her fight-or-flight response, you could say that she was out of her mind.

This is why kabbalists say that when you're angry, you should wait three days before you speak to the person who offended you. By then, you'll be free of the emotion. This might prove more difficult in a romantic relationship, so I'm not suggesting you avoid your partner for three days, but you might choose not to address the issue until the emotion has passed. Then, with a clear mind, if it still bothers you, you can choose to say something or not.

Alternatively, you could make a date to talk about it once you're no longer caught up in the moment, and agree to be civil until things get sorted out. Without the waiting period, it's much more likely that your ego is leading, reacting to whatever upset you. Over time, with practice, the three days will become two and then one, until you don't need so much space before addressing the issues.

The second type of anger is **settled and deliberate,** which often manifests as one partner rejecting the other. It's intentional. A clear example of this can be found in a couple I counseled who had a postnuptial agreement.

This is similar to a pre-nup, but it takes place after the wedding. It was arranged at the wife's behest, even though the couple had children and were fully committed to making the marriage work, yet she felt insecure and decided to take control over the one thing she could. She stood to receive a significant inheritance, and although she was sure her husband hadn't married her solely for her money, she did wonder if that was why he was staying. The post-nup was a reaction to her feeling, and rather than dealing with it proactively, she chose to protect the money she was due to inherit, which was really her way of protecting herself. Three years have passed, and her husband still can't get past the pain of the experience. He reacts by being distant with her, not consistently, but often enough that she feels rejected. At times he is passive-aggressive, emotionally inconsistent, and behaves unfairly. She knows he is capable of better because of the way things used to be, and she sees how well he still treats their children. Her reactivity, which stemmed from the fear of being rejected by him, created an environment in which he felt unsafe and disrespected by her, thus pushing her away. She created exactly what she did not want when she reacted with well thought-out, deliberate anger.

If you're going to get past a hurdle like this, someone has to take the high road. The high road is the only path out of the cyclical nature of reaction and retreat. I suggested she be the one to do so by taking steps to open up more fully to her partner, sharing her reasons for the post-nup, and encouraging him to work through his own pain caused by this issue. I jokingly refer to the high road as the road less traveled, because so few take it. It looks like this: Instead of taking slights personally, even when it feels deliberate, recognize that your partner is acting from pain.

If your partner doesn't immediately want what you're offering, it doesn't mean what you're offering isn't valuable. It just means they aren't willing to accept it right now. Although rejection can lead to a spiral of self-doubt, the objective remains the same. The challenge is not to take it personally.

Here's another approach. When your partner loses his temper, imagine he's a child having a tantrum. I don't mean you should be condescending—quite the opposite. When my youngest was three, she became upset and started screaming, crying, and saying very hurtful things. Anyone could see that she didn't mean them. Instead of reacting to what she was saying, I looked her in the eye and said, "I know you're disappointed." I opened my arms, and she jumped into them. Most of the time, when the people we love are upset and saying hurtful things, all they really want is love and acceptance.

When your partner's words come at you, and you feel like you've been punched in the stomach, try to pause and see if they're acting out of pain. When you want to scream and fight back, that's the moment to compose yourself, practice restriction, and see the wanting behind their words. On the flip side, if you are the person experiencing the anger, it is still in your best interest to put yourself in the other person's shoes. If your goal is for them to understand how you feel, causing them pain is going to bring you the exact opposite of what you're seeking.

The third type is called **dispositional anger,** and this relates more to character, to someone who tends to be very irritable or short-tempered. Knowing your partner's tendency—and your own—can help you develop strategies for handling conflict more effectively.

Ben was a prominent Beverly Hills doctor with a thriving practice, much beloved by his patients. He lived in a beautiful home with his wife and three children. From the outside, he had it all—wealth, respect, and love. But Ben was a rage-aholic. Every day he flew into tantrums so spectacular that it was difficult to believe that anyone could become so angry. Ben died at age 56 of heart failure, which is probably more than a coincidence. Someone who's consistently that angry often suffers from a myriad of health conditions, including high cholesterol or heart disease. Your body can only take so much self-abuse.

Anger in all its forms can be detrimental. Anger is a powerful force, like fire. When disrespected and left unchecked, fire becomes one of the most destructive forces on earth. However, it can also be a wonderful motivator. Rev. Dr. Martin Luther King Jr. used his anger about segregation and unequal rights to change voting laws in this country and to propel the civil rights movement. MADD (Mothers Against Drunk Drivers) was created by Candace Lightner after her thirteen-year-old daughter Cari was killed by a drunk driver. I'm an active advocate for my son Josh because of the challenges that Down syndrome poses for him. When I see that he's being treated unfairly, I use my anger to fight the injustices he faces.

Finding Your Unique Fighting Style

"The difficult part in an argument is not to defend one's opinion, but rather to know it." — Andre Maurois [62]

Q: How did you make your marriage work for 35 years?
A: We never wanted a divorce at the same time.

I get worried when couples don't fight. Fighting has a bad rap, but I've found that it's healthy. In my experience, couples fall into two categories: those who feel passionately enough about their relationship to argue, and those who don't because they have given up. Then "suddenly" (although there is really no such thing as suddenly) a couple who had always looked happy is getting divorced. Believe it or not, there is great importance to fighting and finding your own unique fighting style.

In setting the rules, the first thing we must ask ourselves is: When we fight, what is the outcome we wish to achieve? Is it to feel empowered? To get respect? To be heard? To let your partner know how angry you are? Now ask yourself: does my anger, whether it's expressed as the silent treatment or fits of rage, take me to the outcome I'm looking for? The answer usually is no. Early in our marriage, year four to be specific, Michael and I discovered our fighting style. The style that I had been using was one of escalation. I would get upset about something small, and the feeling grew and grew until I was ablaze with anger. It often had nothing at all to do with what we were fighting about. It was based on a lot of other frustrations. Whereas Michael completely shut down. What we did agree on was that neither style was working. We came up with a plan to handle future conflicts in a way we both felt comfortable with.

There is one cardinal rule which should always be honored during an argument, and that is to never hit below the belt. There are some things you just don't say without risking serious damage to the relationship. "You're acting like your mother, and I hate her!" falls into that category. Other examples include wishing bad things on your partner, calling them names, or cursing the day they were born. Michael and I do argue, but the argument never hits below the belt, and it always encompasses human dignity. We discuss, we don't yell, and we speak from a vulnerable, open place. We're honest about what we're feeling, and we try to use "I" statements rather than "you" statements. Our fighting style looks something like this. We preface the discussion with, "I really hope you can hear what I'm saying. I'm not trying to hurt you. I just want to express what is on my mind." We trust each other with our vulnerabilities, and therefore when we argue, it's safe to discuss how we feel and express ourselves without the fear of judgment or being punished later. This takes years of practice, but it can be done. It first starts with the intention to set your relationship up this way. At this point, we know each other so well that in the middle of a fight, we break down laughing, or stick our tongues out at each other. Our levity melts any feelings of ill will.

Too often though, each person may position themselves to win, becoming focused on how hurt they feel and proving that they are right and their spouse is wrong. Eventually, the lines of communication break down, or worse, the couple may emotionally shut down altogether. Every comment and vulnerability becomes fair game when an argument escalates. As it says in Proverbs12:18, "Reckless words pierce like a sword, but the tongue of the wise brings healing." Past mistakes are too often used against each other, and oneness and intimacy can be shattered. A hurt individual may tell any lie (or omit important facts or details, which is really the same thing) that occurs to them in order to position themselves "to win." In reality, they are setting themselves up to win the battle, but lose the war.

Here's an example of how Michael and I once avoided a fight altogether. Along with our youngest daughter, the two of us drove to Pennsylvania to visit our two middle kids at sleep-away camp. We had a lot of fun seeing our teenagers, but it was a very long day. So on the way home, not only were we tired, but we all felt grimy. You know that layer of dirt that sticks to the layer of sunscreen, and in between all of the layers, you have been sweating? I couldn't wait to get in the shower. Then the traffic on the way home was brutal, turning a three-hour drive into a five-hour journey, and on top of it all, our three-year-old got carsick. So now, factor in vomit with fatigue, grime, and frustration.

Is it any wonder that my Waze app navigator, Jane, started to get on my nerves? (In my defense, she's incredibly bossy.) That's when I discovered "boy band" navigation. If you haven't tried it, I implore you to do so. This setting sings directions. Think Justin Timberlake crooning "Turrrrn left, turrrrrn left. In half a mile turn riiiiight, then turn riiiight." Next thing I knew I was laughing so hard the long-distance drive didn't seem so bad or nearly as daunting. My husband and I tried all the options available and, as Hebrew and Farsi speakers, we came up with a few creative options ourselves—think 'Boy Band: Middle Eastern Edition.'

We've all been in situations where we're on the verge. Something's gotta give. And in fact, something does, but we get to choose which way it goes. We can snap, be reactive, lash out, sulk, or blame other people for our situation. *Or*, we can have some fun. We are all prone to anger and frustration. The truth is, giving in to anger is easy. There is a feeling of satisfaction when we let ourselves vent and rage. But that satisfaction is short-term and inevitably leaves us in a worse mood than we were to begin with. The harder—but far more rewarding—choice is to look for the good in the situation. Think of it as a secret door; it may be hidden, but every situation has one. We find it through perspective, kindness, and consciousness.

There are many different styles of conflict. Here are some questions to ask yourself in order to discover your fighting style as a couple. If you're single, reflect on a past relationship or fights you may have had with close friends or family members. Our fighting style in a relationship often mirrors the way we fight with other people we are close with.

Rethink Moment

- **How do you fight? How does your partner fight?**

- **Think about the last argument you had with your loved one. How did you express yourself?**

- **How did the fight impact the relationship?**

- **If you could do it all over again, what approach would you take? What approach do you wish your partner had taken?**

No single fighting style is better than another. The key is that the fighting style you choose has to work for both of you. A marriage's failure to do this will sadly cause a husband and wife to find themselves in useless arguments, which will eventually lead to them becoming isolated in their marriage.

Here are ten baseline rules of engagement for effective fighting:

1. Discuss lines that neither of you should ever cross. No hitting below the belt.

2. Agree on a fighting style that works for both of you. Whether you choose to vent, or sit and discuss calmly, the style has to accommodate both of your needs.

3. Identify in advance what an acceptable outcome looks like.

4. Assign the time of day you are most open to hearing each other.

5. Avoid overreacting. Remain open enough to see your partner's perspective

6. Discuss one issue at a time, and be specific. Don't use this as an opportunity to rehash the many grievances that have come up in the history of your relationship. Stick to the issue at hand, not about what happened last week or five years ago.

7. Avoid words like "always" and "never." These are trigger words that escalate arguments.

8. Don't interrupt. Take turns speaking. Listen actively, with the intention of really hearing what the other person has to say.

9. Be willing to compromise. We all have things that are important to us. When it's very important to your partner, see where you can be more flexible. Take turns compromising.

10. A successful fight means you both walk away feeling heard and understood. Remember, it is not about winning.

Ultimately, if you don't feel appreciated, heard, or have open lines of communication, then these "petty" fights that occur usually aren't what you're fighting about at all. It isn't about the remote, or going to the in-laws' for dinner, and it certainly isn't about the toilet seat being left up. But it's going to be difficult to get to the underlying issues unless you agree upon a fighting style and rules of engagement.

When the Anxious Meet the Avoidant, Nobody Feels Secure

There are three attachment styles: avoidant, anxious, and secure. Being aware of your attachment style helps you understand why you fight the way you do. Usually, attachment styles begin with mom. From a purely biological point of view, forming a deep bond between mother and infant is important for the very survival of the child. As the child develops, the type of relationship that the mother and child have will vary dramatically and have a lasting impact on the way we behave in adult relationships. There are many factors that contribute to your attachment style, including relationships with role models, teachers, and partners.

Lynn and Connor were very much in love, but their interactions were fraught with conflict. While both were capable of having a secure, intimate relationship based on love and respect, they seemed to be incapable of keeping even the slightest disagreement from becoming a huge argument. Every battle became personal and grew to include a long list of historical grievances on each side.

Lynn is a very warm, open, and naturally loving person, and the way she attempted to make her husband happy was to accommodate his needs. She's a people pleaser. However, when her own needs went unmet, she became very unhappy. She began to take everything personally and spun even innocuous comments into negative ones. When her insecurity peaked, she withdrew, but in a way that was calculated to get Connor's attention.

Her pattern is to:
- Please him
- Become unhappy
- Spin out of control
- Repeat.

This is the very definition of a vicious cycle!

In this example, Lynn's attachment style was anxious. Connor, on the other hand, was a classic avoidant. He created distance and prized independence over reliance on others. He could be intimate, but he preferred not to share his feelings. While married, he maintained the illusion of freedom by being dissatisfied and thus created emotional distance. He often focused on Lynn's flaws and idealized his life before marriage, believing that a different woman would have been a more suitable wife. From his perspective, all of her attempts at closeness looked like attempts to control or manipulate him. The more she yearned for closeness, the more avoidant he became which manifested in behaviors that created even more distance, such as flirting with others, unilateral decision making, or a refusal to share even insignificant details about his day-to-day routines.

The needier Lynn felt, the stronger and more self-sufficient Connor felt. But this was all an act on his part. What he wanted was connection and closeness with his wife. He only pretended that he didn't need her love and affection. The danger in this is that if you lie to yourself consistently, you begin to believe the lie is true.

I've described avoidant and anxious, and the third attachment style is secure. A person with a secure attachment style doesn't play games. They are comfortable sharing their needs, thoughts, and desires, and are respectful and supportive of their partner's. They forgive easily, and when conflict arises, they focus on problem-solving rather than winning. Secure people form deep bonds based on interdependence, not co-dependence.

Studies estimate that 50% of people have a secure attachment style, while 20% are anxious, and 25% are avoidant. [63]

People who had avoidant parents may emulate that style, or because they were desperate for their parents' love, they may become anxious in their attachment behaviors. Unfortunately, people with an anxious attachment style will often be attracted to avoidants, while being disinterested in someone with a secure attachment style. Even though these relationships are uncomfortable and anxiety-inducing, they are familiar and therefore, perceived as safe. Often, those with anxious attachment styles hold beliefs of not being good enough or lovable. On the other hand, distancers, those with avoidant attachment styles, love being pursued. It sustains them emotionally. Being in a relationship with another distancer would prove completely emotionally unsatisfying.

If any of this is hitting too close to home, know that with conscious effort, you can change your behaviors.

Rethink Moment

The list of suggestions below will help you cultivate secure attachments.

- **Know your worth. You are lovable, and you deserve to be loved. You were sent to this world with a unique purpose, one that only you can fulfill.**

- **Identify, and then ask for what you really want. Repressing your true desires confuses your partner and leaves you with feelings of lack.**

- **Be honest and fair. Do not play games.**

- **Do not become a fault finder. Judgment invites more judgment. Whether you are judging yourself or your partner, you will find that the judgments begin to multiply. Conversely, giving someone the benefit of the doubt or treating yourself with mercy, invites more mercy into your life.**

- **Stop reacting. Every time we act or speak, we have a choice. We can say or do positive things, or we can make things worse.**

- **Learn to see issues as not happening to you, but rather happening to us. Some of the strongest couples I know approach life from the perspective of "we."**

There are always plenty of things to disagree about. It's important to remember that no story tells exactly what went on from all points of view. There are always three sides to a story: her side, his side, and the truth.

Chapter Nineteen

I'm Sorry

KABBALISTIC PRINCIPLE:

Anything damaged can be restored when we take
responsibility for the harm we have caused others.

. . . .

Tshuva is a Hebrew word that means repentance, but it is much more than
that. Tshuva involves taking a hard look at the past and taking stock of
your missteps, those instances where you were reactive and may have
hurt someone. It is not a simple inventory of gaffes, mistakes, errors, or
moments of poor judgments. Tshuva literally means "return," and it acts
like a cosmic eraser; it is an opportunity for renewal that can be incredibly
powerful within relationships. Tshuva is much more than saying, I'm sorry.
Rav Berg put it this way, "To say I'm sorry is not enough. If someone steps
on my foot, he says, 'I'm sorry, forgive me.' One may think, 'You're not
forgiven... You're just saying you're sorry. My foot still hurts. What does
your sorry have to do with it? Restore my foot so that it doesn't hurt me.'"

I love that explanation from Rav Berg, as it demonstrates that regret alone
is simply not enough. It doesn't remove any pain we've caused.

If you're anything like me, there are deeds that you wish you hadn't done,
words you'd prefer had remained unspoken, thoughts you wish you'd left
unconsidered, along with some opportunities you would rather have taken.
We dredge up all this unpleasantness because the damage can be corrected,
not because we like to beat ourselves over the head with our past mistakes,
but because of the opportunity self-reflection brings us to transform our
life and our relationships.

There are six aspects of tshuva:

1. **Review Your Errors** Benjamin Franklin once said, "The history of errors of mankind, all things considered, is more valuable and interesting than that of their discoveries." Acknowledging our errors allows us to make adjustments, and to have empathy for others who are making mistakes. Being wrong is a vital part of how we learn and change. Every time we make a mistake, we have a new opportunity to revise our understanding of ourselves, our partner, and the world at large.

Compiling areas that need review and acknowledging behavior that is not of our highest selves can be difficult. We need to see ourselves as we are—the good, the bad, and the ugly—no matter how painful that assessment may be. Your partner can be a great help here. Ask him or her this question: "What do you think I most need to change about myself?"

Remain open and prepare yourself to hear whatever they say without fear. You're just looking for feedback here, collecting data points for further analysis. Their response contains precious gifts for you, gems of insight that can ultimately take you both to a place of growth and fulfillment. If you want to push yourself even further, seek out a person for whom you have deep respect. They are perhaps not a close friend or confidante, but with a little explanation, reach out, and ask them the same question. Once again settle your mind and prepare to receive some information. Is this practice uncomfortable? Yes. Illuminating, even more so.

2. **Practice Empathy** Put yourself in your partner's shoes and relive the experience through their eyes. This means there is no defensiveness or justification of your error. Interestingly, it turns out that we're all hardwired for empathy. We have neurons in our prefrontal cortex that fire when we throw a ball, and these same neurons fire in exactly the same way when we see someone else throwing a ball. These are called "mirror neurons," and scientists believe they form the biological basis of empathy. When an infant hears another baby cry, it will begin to cry. This is our first experience identifying with others—walking the proverbial mile in someone else's shoes.

Empathy allows us to cultivate an understanding of our partner's feelings so we can behave toward them the way that we would want to be treated (or even better than we'd treat ourselves).

3. **Cultivate Compassion** Empathy leads to compassion, which Merriam-Webster defines as "sympathetic consciousness of others' distress together with a desire to alleviate it." Compassion is empathy in action. As adults, it is sometimes difficult to awaken empathy because as we grow up, experiences in which we've been hurt or disappointed can easily teach us to be suspicious of others' motivation or keep their troubling experiences at arm's length.

Without being sensitive to the needs and emotions of others, our relationships lack depth. Compassion allows us to form genuine bonds. Narcissists, for example, tend to think that only their feelings are important, and have a poorly developed sense of empathy. This makes their interactions with others superficial and largely unfulfilling for everyone involved. It is so important to catch ourselves when we display behaviors, such as selfish thoughts, or begin to keep score in our relationships. When we shift our focus away from giving and from empathy, we begin to grow our feelings of lack and resentment. What we give our energy to grows.

Our love and empathy have the power to alleviate the suffering of others.

There is a parable about a man whose son was given a terminal diagnosis. Not wanting to accept this as fact, he decided to visit his mentor, and the two men prayed together. With deep sadness, the mentor told him that there was, in fact, nothing anyone could do. Heartbroken, the man went on his way. As soon as he left, the mentor realized that there was something that he could do. He dashed after the man, overtaking him on the road. "I realized after you left that if I can't help your son, the least I can do is cry with you." So, the two men sat down side by side and wept together. This is the essence of compassion, to feel the pain of others just as deeply as if it were your own; on a spiritual level, all the pain in the world is shared. For most people, compassion is conditional. If your partner is sharing and loving, you find it easy to respond in kind. But compassion is most called for when you least feel like giving it. In those times, some may snap, "Why are you acting like that? What's your problem?" When someone pushes my buttons by speaking in a condescending way, I encourage myself to think, "This is the best they can do; inadequate though it may be, it's their best effort." That allows my heart to open.

Compassion calls for a release of all judgments. Without judgment, compassion can be felt for those with whom you would not have found it possible—those who cheat, steal, harm others, who are mean-spirited, stingy, or embittered. You may be asking yourself why you would want to feel compassion for people like that. But who among us is perfect? And what happened in their lives that made them become that way? The scary truth is that we have more in common with such people than we want to believe.

"Make no judgments where you have no compassion." — Anne McCaffrey [64]

4. **Connect to Your Highest Self** The soul is never damaged, only covered by our negative actions. Therefore, our soul (our perfect self) remains untarnished and accessible. Most of us are nowhere near living as our perfect self. To do so, we have to believe in our own perfection! It's impossible to connect to something that you don't believe even exists. Most of us don't have any idea what our true potential may be, and without that clarity, how will we ever attain it? As the proverb says: "If you don't know where you're going, you're never going to get there."

Before anything comes into existence, it is preceded by a moment of perfection. Kabbalist Rav Ashlag compares this to an architect who wants to build a beautiful house. In the moment of inspiration when he comes up with the idea for the house he wants to build (or in our case, when we first think of anything we wish to create), contained in that insight is the full, magnificent perfection of that creation. However imperfect that final house may be, the thought that preceded construction was perfect. The skylight didn't leak. Water didn't pool on the laundry room floor. In much the same way, the Creator had a vision of creation that included every soul that will come into this world. His intention was not the state we are in now, but a perfect version of ourselves. Our job now is to find that perfect self, and we do this through the work of tshuva, by returning to that perfected state initially envisioned for us.

5. **Forgive, Repair, Repeat** There's no playbook for forgiving, no manual for getting past betrayals, disappointments, and hurts. Forgiveness is a simple concept; it's the execution that's hard. Author Kathryn Schulz explains, "It's wrongness, not rightness, that can teach us who we are. The experience of being right is imperative for our survival, and it gratifies our ego." [65] But in a culture that associates error with shame, stupidity, and ignorance, the idea of error seems like death. Basically, we're wrong about what it means to be wrong. Maybe that's why it's so difficult to forgive. Our ego steps in and doesn't allow us to forgive even though we know that holding onto the hurt is harmful.

"The weak can never forgive. Forgiveness is the attribute of the strong."
— Mahatma Gandhi [66]

To forgive requires honesty, humility, commitment, generosity, and courage. Often we expect people who really wronged us to ask us for forgiveness. But some people don't have these characteristics, nor do they even have the capacity to seek forgiveness. If they did, they wouldn't have committed the act in the first place.

Once you understand this, forgiveness for those who have wronged you becomes easier. We make it about that 'awful' person and feel hatred towards them when that enemy is actually a blessing pushing us toward greatness. This can transform vengeance into gratitude. It's not about the other person. It's about us.

There's a story from the Zohar that illustrates this point, which I'd like to share. Rav Aba saw a traveler standing near the edge of a cliff on the mountainside. The man must have been weary because he lay down on the side of the road and fell asleep. While he was asleep, a snake came toward him, but then a larger snake suddenly appeared and killed the smaller snake. The disruption woke the traveler, startled by the large snake, he stepped back from the edge of the cliff. Just then, the rock ledge he'd just been sleeping on sheared away and plunged to the valley below, leaving him shaken but unharmed. If he had awoken a moment later, or not seen the snake, he would have fallen to his death. Rav Aba approached the traveler and said, "Who are you, and what have you done that the two miracles were performed for you: first saving you from the snake, and then saving you from the falling mountainside? Surely these events did not happen without a reason."

The traveler thought for a moment and replied. "In all my days, I forgave and made peace with any man who did evil by me. If I could not make peace with him, I did not go to sleep before forgiving him. I did not harbor hatred for any harm that was done to me. Moreover, I tried to do kindness by those who had aggrieved me."

As important as it is to forgive, reparation is equally vital. Many couples know how to exit an argument, but happy couples know how to repair the situation after an argument ensues. Reparation is a necessary step because without sorting through all the feelings involved and getting a sense of how the other person felt, it's difficult to come up with a heartfelt apology. Coming back together to repair through discussion and apologies keeps a relationship evolving.

Without repair, fighting becomes the primary theme of the marriage. The words "I'm sorry," when combined with the five other steps in tshuva, can repair a broken relationship, but how an apology is worded matters. There are good and bad apologies. Bad apologies include justifying your behavior, blaming the other person, making excuses, and minimizing the other person's feelings. "I'm sorry you feel this way," is not a good apology. An effective apology has to include the words "I'm sorry that I." Take responsibility for the mistake, actively seek a way to make amends, make a commitment to behave differently in the future and ask for forgiveness. You actually must say these three words: "Please forgive me." When you say those words, you put your ego on the line. It is a humbling experience, and this humility is necessary for tshuva to be effective.

6. **Let It Go...** The final step is to let it go completely. This may sound simple, but forgiving ourselves and others is no small task. I find so many people stuck in their past errors and unable to move beyond them. Conversely, others are stuck waiting for an apology that will never come.

"To forgive is to set a prisoner free and discover that the prisoner was you."
— Lewis B. Smedes [67]

188

Chapter Twenty

Awakening Appreciation

Among my favorite movies are *The Bridges of Madison County, The Notebook, Pride and Prejudice,* and *Dirty Dancing*–all epic love stories. As viewers, we go out into the world looking to recreate that cinematic passion with another person, and maybe we do. Over time, when we don't have as strong a connection with our partner, we may get distracted by the potential "perfect" others we see outside the relationship, which creates a lack of appreciation. When we focus on what we lack, we endanger the good things in our lives. The reason relationships falter is not usually because of a lack of feeling on each person's part. The number one reason a marriage dies is because neither spouse recognizes the value of the relationship until it's too late. As Rav Berg said, "The moment appreciation is lost, the relationship is lost." [68]

On a cold January morning, a man at a metro station in Washington, D.C. started to play the violin. He played six Bach pieces for about 45 minutes. Since it was rush hour, thousands of people passed through the station. A few slowed briefly to listen, and after several minutes the violinist received his first tip. A woman threw a dollar in his till as she dashed past. The one who paid the most attention was a 3-year-old boy. His mother dragged him along, hurried, but the kid stopped to look at the violinist. Finally, the mother pulled hard, and the child continued to walk, turning his head all the while. Several other children repeated this action. All the parents, without exception, forced them to move on. Only six people stopped and listened for a while. The violinist collected $32. When he finished playing, no one noticed. No one applauded, nor was there any recognition. The violinist was Joshua Bell, one of the top musicians in the world. [69] That day he played one of the most intricate pieces ever written for the violin on a Stradivarius worth 3.5 million dollars.

Two days before, Joshua Bell had sold out at a theater in Boston where the average seat cost $100. He was playing incognito in the metro station as part of a social experiment about perception. Because people didn't have a way to judge the value of what they were hearing, most of them failed to appreciate it.

Do You Stop to Appreciate the World Around You?

Most people consider themselves grateful for the good things in their lives. However, when we lose appreciation for those things, we no longer see their value. By contrast, when we're grateful, we take it to another level, feeling overwhelming gratitude for simply being alive and being loved. All of us, to greater and lesser degrees, fail at having a consistent and accurate appreciation for our gifts. To put it in perspective, your odds of ever being born were 1 in 400 trillion, and every morning that you wake up is an improbable and beautiful gift.

Many of the most exceptional relationships were forged through challenges. For example, couples who survived the instability of World War II have a great appreciation for each other. Putting this in perspective, it's understandable why. When soldiers saw men, women, and children dying around them daily, it became effortless to appreciate their loved ones, even through difficult times.

Looking at a more recent event, the crisis of 9/11 had the same effect. In effect, a crisis creates a sense of urgency that immediately puts our relationships in the right order on our list of priorities. A crisis awakens a greater appreciation for life, increases personal strength, and leads to warmer and more intimate relationships, changed priorities, spiritual development, and the recognition of new possibilities. In layman's terms: when something horrible happens, you can become better for it and more appreciative for your blessings in life, namely your partner.

However, you don't need to be in a crisis to cultivate appreciation. When one couple I know gets in an argument, they turn to one another and say,

"Imagine there was a gun to our heads." Once they visualize that, all the pettiness of the argument is removed and is replaced with appreciation and love.

I've seen couples who are great in a crisis but implode when things are calm. To me, this seems like such a waste. The times when things are calm is like a free pass when couples can experience the rewards of their relationship. Couples who continuously bicker when there is no real crisis usually do so because they are bored and they've lost appreciation. If a couple can get along during difficult times, then they can get along in calm times. I cannot emphasize strongly enough to take advantage of the times without significant challenges, because these are the free passes of life.

From Worthless to Priceless

Although we have many wonderful things in our lives, it's human nature to focus on one or two areas in which we believe we're lacking.

To avoid falling into this frame of mind, take this two-step approach:

- **Step 1:** Beware of the ego, which pesters us about what we don't have and everything wrong in our relationship.

- **Step 2:** Resist the tendency to take things for granted. Tell yourself, "I'm not going to focus on those few areas where things could be better. I'm going to reawaken my appreciation for all the things that are going well."

When my first child, David, was born, my appreciation for his mere existence was overwhelming. The touch of his mouth on my neck, the smell of his skin, his delicate skull with a head of hair that stood straight up, cradled in my hand. Any sound he uttered was heavenly. Now, he's at that stage of his young adulthood where he's quick to point out things he dislikes. Naturally, some of his criticism is directed at me, and I find my appreciation is underwhelming at times even though my love hasn't changed.

When he was 14 years old, David dashed toward me enthusiastically announcing, "Aba (Dad) is coming to my baseball game tomorrow, and he's going to record it for you to watch!" He eagerly added, "Will you watch the video, Mom?" I responded with what I thought would be good news, that I wouldn't need to watch the video because I could come to his game, too. He shifted from one foot to the other, his eyes restless as he scanned the room, desperate to avoid making eye contact with me. Looking away, he muttered, "It might be a better idea if just Aba comes to my baseball game, and he can record it for you." I turned to him, perplexed. "But I can come, David, there's no need to videotape it." He just repeated himself in a soft voice, "No, no. That's ok. Aba will record it for you."

I eventually discovered that my eight-month-pregnant existence was a little embarrassing for him in front of his friends (who, at that age, knew how babies were made). While I knew he didn't mean to hurt my feelings, my ego was a little bruised. I wasn't overtly upset, but I did quickly announce that it was time for bed. When my thoughts, words, and actions come from a place of the ego, my ability to access love is compromised. In that moment when David, without intention, rejected me, I felt angry and created space between us. Some situations arise that make us lack appreciation for our loved ones, and thankfully there are times that awaken renewed appreciation, and then the love comes rushing back.

When you appreciate your partner, you're keenly aware of things that could come between the two of you, and therefore, steer clear of them. For instance, for the sake of transparency, one person in the relationship might say, "I want you to know that I'm attracted to somebody at work, but it doesn't mean anything. I love you." But it does mean something. The words themselves create an opening, a little gulf that opens up between you. Sometimes even having a trainer or a massage therapist of the opposite sex can create that little rift, because it encourages physical intimacy with a person outside the relationship. How comfortable are you with having another person touching your or your partner's body? If you have an appreciation for your partner, you try very hard to leave no room for any kind of opening. You may notice that someone is attractive, but you can choose not to fantasize about them, or put yourself in a situation where something might actually happen between you.

KABBALISTIC PRINCIPLE:

Appreciation is a spiritual force that
helps to protect all that we have.

· · · · · · · ·

Appreciation is a choice we make, a switch that we hit in our minds. Social scientists report that people who make a practice of writing down just one thing a day that they are grateful for show a marked rise in happiness—in less than a month.[70] That's a small investment with a big pay-off. Write down one thing each day that you appreciate about your partner. You'll be amazed at the positive effect this can have on your relationship. Then, if you want to take this a step further, take a moment each day to share that appreciative feeling with your partner.

Very often we complain about what we're not getting, and how we're not supported by our partner, when, in fact, we're not supported because we don't appreciate who they are; it's not the other way around.

We've touched upon a kabbalistic theme again. If you want something, first give it.

"Great secrets are not those that are difficult to understand, but rather difficult to do."— Rav Ashlag

Think of your relationship like a farm that provides you with fruits and vegetables time and time again, and you take from it repeatedly. But imagine if you never go back to tend to it, replant seeds, fertilize it, water it, or nurture it. Is it going to keep providing for you? No, it's going to dry up. We want to become an appreciator rather than a depreciator for everything in our lives.

Chapter Twenty One

Allowing Yourself to Be Known

KABBALISTIC PRINCIPLE:

Real union only comes from knowledge of one another.

. . . .

Kabbalists explain that real union only comes from knowledge of one another. Interestingly, the biblical term for sexual love is "to know." The Bible says, "Adam knew Eve, and she became pregnant." Most of us crave to be completely known by someone and to build a committed relationship based on honesty, trust, self-disclosure, respect, and togetherness. Getting to know your partner deeply leads to higher levels of intimacy and a greater sense of love.

Will You Read My Mind?

We've established how difficult it is to know what is going on in our minds at any given moment. Yet, we somehow expect our partners to know our thoughts before we even express them, sort of like, "Hey, Babe, will you read my mind?" Even worse, we assume we know what our partner is thinking, so we don't bother to find out. Perhaps Henry Winkler, otherwise known as The Fonz on "Happy Days," put it best when he said, "Assumptions are the termites of relationships." [71]

Throughout my years of counseling, I've worked with couples whose relationships are high on the emotionally intelligent spectrum. Being emotionally intelligent means understanding and taking responsibility

195

for our feelings and the situations we find ourselves in. When you are emotionally intelligent, you can use emotions as data. This data unearths the root source of sadness, anger, or frustration and why emotions change and escalate seemingly without warning. Emotionally intelligent couples keep their negative thoughts and feelings about each other (which all couples have) from overwhelming their positive ones.

To be emotionally intelligent in a relationship is to know each other's worlds in great detail, starting from childhood to current experiences. It means you know your partner's history even before you were in the picture (even exes!) You know each other's feelings about your respective bosses. If you visit your spouse at work, you would recognize the receptionist, know where the coffee machine is located, and where they hide the creamer. You would never tease your husband about his lack of athleticism if he had, for example, been labeled a 'fat kid' growing up and worked very hard to overcome his weight challenges. You learn what shaped them into the people they are today and into the person that you fell in love with. In the beginning of every relationship, we ask a lot of questions. Don't forget to continue doing so throughout the entirety of your relationship.

Dr. John Gottman posits that the opposite of the emotionally intelligent couple is the disengaged couple, who are "marked by the absence of positive affect during conflict (no interest, affection, humor, or empathy)." [72] A perfect example of this is when our partner is stressed or acting odd, and we have no idea why, so we take it personally.

Early in my marriage, before my husband and I were emotionally intelligent, we argued. It was so long ago I can't recall the specifics, but what I do remember is that he said, "That's just crazy!" Take note that he didn't call *me* crazy, but he used "crazy" in a sentence in relation to me, and I became enraged.

Not quite the reaction you would think someone would have to such an innocuous, and might I add common, marital exchange. It would not be the worst insult in the world, even if he had called me crazy. However, had my husband known my history, he would have known that my uncle is schizophrenic and that one of my greatest childhood fears was that I would somehow suffer my uncle's fate. Emotionally intelligent couples know how to avoid these outbursts, because their respective pasts are known to their partners, and handled with care and empathy. Once Michael knew the story, he never used that word again in an argument.

Vulnerability

Sharing our past fears, traumas, and embarrassments require vulnerability and openness. This isn't easy because we fear that our vulnerability will be construed as weakness. But by opening yourself to your partner, you create a safe space in which you both become stronger together—stronger than you could ever be apart.

Emotional intelligence gives way to an even deeper facet of the relationship. The active ingredient here is self-revelation. The more you get to know somebody, assuming you feel safe and understood, the more you start revealing about yourself. In a successful relationship, both partners make themselves known, gradually disclosing their innermost selves, divulging their desires, fears, fantasies, and dreams–even those that don't show them in the most favorable light.

Vulnerability is opening yourself up to possibly being physically or emotionally wounded. Admittedly, vulnerability sounds distinctly unpleasant. Terrifying, even.

In dysfunctional relationships, it can be painful to be vulnerable because the disclosures will most likely be used against you in the heat of a future argument. Vulnerability at its best creates such deep connection that when you walk in a room and look at your significant other—just by a look—you know what the other is thinking, feeling and what kind of day they've had. Regardless of circumstance, you feel completely accepted and embraced in every sense of the word. You understand each other so completely, it's as if you are experiencing the same emotion. The rewards of vulnerability far outweigh the risk. You may wonder at this point how to become vulnerable, well, here's another secret: being vulnerable isn't a choice. You're already vulnerable every single day of your life.

Different Ways Men and Women Express Intimacy

You may be familiar with Maslow's hierarchy of needs, which he proposed in 1943.[73] They're often seen as a triangle with the most fundamental needs forming the base and the loftiest at the pinnacle. Maslow's hierarchy consists of:

1. Physical needs (air, water, food, shelter, sleep)
2. Safety (primarily physical safety)
3. Love/Belonging
4. Esteem
5. Self-actualization

Maslow posits that all human motivation is based on filling one of these needs. Many of us have food and water, a roof over our heads, and feel safe in our daily lives. Once those desires are fulfilled, we move higher up the pyramid to seeking love and a sense of belonging, to then exploring our talents and interests, and finally to the striving for self-actualization, in other words, working to meet our greatest potential. Meeting these needs is a lifelong process—it's integral to our happiness and having fulfilling relationships.

While both men and women crave the intimacy that comes with Maslow's third stage, love and belonging, how they express their desire can manifest in different ways.

Intimacy requires being in your comfort zone, and what makes men and women comfortable can differ considerably.

When women want to draw closer to one another, they face each other, lock eyes, and anchor their gaze (which conveys being fully engaged), before revealing their innermost feelings, aspirations, and concerns. Women also read emotion by maintaining eye contact. Men, on the other hand, tend to display intimacy while positioned side-by-side—usually while working or playing together. For one thing, this keeps them aware of other stimuli in the environment. For another, direct eye contact between men can be interpreted as hostile or challenging.

Men might discuss a lousy week at work with each other, or troubles in their love lives, but they rarely share their secret hopes for the future or their darkest fears. If they do, they often camouflage it with humor, and they rarely look deeply into another's eyes. This goes back to ancestral times when they faced down their enemies, but sat next to their friends. This reminds me of my oldest son, David, playing video games with his friends. They sit side by side for hours. It may not look like it, but they're bonding. Before I understood this, I was struck by the strangeness of seeing a room full of boys playing video games, seemingly not interacting with each other. I didn't see the value in it. This looked like something that David could do by himself—and more quietly, I might add.

Because it is difficult for men to have emotional intimacy with other men, it's doubly important that the relationship that a man has with his partner allows him to express his desires in every area—physically, emotionally, sexually, and spiritually. In counseling couples, I have seen some men cheat when they don't feel their partners care to understand how they feel. When that intimacy is missing from their relationship, men tend to seek it elsewhere. When it comes to desire, men express this very differently, as well, but, for most women, it comes more naturally to express emotions. Many women make the mistake of not realizing how difficult it is for men to express themselves, and when they do, women often do not take them seriously enough. If both people in the relationship are aware of these differences in intimacy styles, there will be more opportunities to deepen intimacy.

Studies conducted by psychologist Jay Carter illustrate that a child's most important developmental period is the first five years of his life. [74] During those formative years, boys get a sense of their self-esteem from their mothers. Boys have a greater propensity to want to make their mothers proud. Carter explains that in later years as men, this desire to be becoming to their mother is transferred onto the women they meet, date, and marry. This essentially means that a man's self-esteem is incredibly vulnerable when it comes to a woman's opinion of him. We place far too much importance on what other people think of us. In this case, knowing this about men can prove incredibly helpful for women when trying to navigate the relationship.

A lot of times, women criticize their husbands, boyfriends, and brothers, (and sometimes even their fathers) without being fully aware of the negative impact it can have on them. Men take words more literally than women, and therefore, take criticism as a sweeping statement. If a woman calls her husband irresponsible for leaving clothes all over the floor, he hears that she thinks he is irresponsible in all areas. In his mind, he starts to think about all the responsible things he's done that she seems to have forgotten. She doesn't realize he thinks this way and so over time if she keeps speaking this way, he starts to dismiss her and all of her requests. When men feel repeatedly criticized, it results in them pulling further away and shutting down altogether, quite the opposite of the original goal.

Women tend not to realize what kind of influence they actually have over the men in their lives. There is a healthier way to appeal to a man that doesn't need to come in the form of criticism. If women can understand how men process their words, then they can deliver their messages without dealing a massive blow to a man's self-esteem. For instance, she can say 'I see how organized you are with your golf clubs, it would be great if you could be as mindful of your clothes, as well.'

"All men make mistakes, but married men find out about them sooner."
— Red Skelton [75]

I'm not suggesting that all women are savvier about emotions and have better people skills than men. There are plenty of women who are insensitive. But women do tend to be more emotionally aware than men for one simple reason. They have an enormous head start in acquiring these skills. John Gottman noted that when you observe children at any playground, young boys usually run around and chase each other.[76] Their priority is the game, not their relationship with one another. Whereas, when little girls are engaged in an activity together, feelings are paramount. A cry of "I'm not your friend anymore!" can bring a game to a screeching halt, and whether the game starts up again depends on whether or not the girls make up.

Even when a boy and girl play with the same toy, the gender difference is apparent. Gottman observed four-year-old best friends Naomi and Erik sharing a baby doll. Naomi wanted to pretend that the doll was their baby, and they were going to show it off to their friends (relationship-based play). Erik went along with this for about ten minutes before he shifted the game into more comfortable territory. "Hey, Naomi. This baby is dead," he announced. "We have to get it to the hospital right away!" Erik climbed into the pretend ambulance with the baby, and away he went, while Naomi urged him not to drive too fast. Suddenly they both became surgeons and saved the baby doll's life (although Erik did want Naomi to be the nurse). Once the baby was okay, both children went back to showing off the baby to their friends.

The play styles of Naomi and Erik are equally charming and delightful, but the truth is girlish games offer far more preparation for marriage and family life because they focus on relationships. Conversely, boys' play doesn't. Think about it. While no preschool dress-up corner would be complete without bridal costumes, you never see tuxedos for little pretend grooms.

This difference in conditioning is heightened by the fact that as they get older, boys rarely play with girls, so they miss the chance to learn from each other.

Gottman continues with some interesting statistics:
- Although 35% of preschool best friends are boys and girls like Naomi and Erik, by age seven that percentage plummets to virtually zero.
- From age seven to puberty, the sexes will have little or nothing to do with each other.
- From age seven until puberty, our culture offers no formal structure for ensuring that boys and girls continue to interact. [77]

By the time Naomi and Erik are grown, the difference in their knowledge of how to be emotionally intimate will be significant. Once a couple moves in together, they're plunging themselves into an alien world. That world will continue to look foreign to them if they aren't actively sharing, reviewing, and revealing new things about themselves.

201

The other day I walked into my husband's office and said, "You know honey, there's something that you don't know about me." He looked at me as though he knew what I was going to say, but he ended up being surprised. "Sometimes, when I have a craving for sugar, I eat the kids' vitamins. So, I get some calcium, and it tastes like a gummy bear!" Why did I share this with him? Because it's about being intimate in many different ways. It's about sharing as you discover something new about yourself. This revelation may seem mundane, but he already knows the juicier, richer facts. The point is that the things I discover about myself, I continually share with Michael, and he does the same with me. This self-disclosure is what keeps people close.

Even after 22 years of marriage, every once in a while, I will still share something with him, and he'll say, "Oh, that's new!" In those moments, I feel closest to him because he knows me, and I know him. We practice transparency. We let ourselves be seen.

Chapter Twenty Two

Rethink Sex

Circuitry between male and female energies is what creates fulfillment in a relationship. Men and women each have specific—and complementary—energetic roles. Kabbalistically, men are the sharing energy, or conduit for the Light, while women are the receiving energy or vessel for the Light. Female energy supports and directs where a man reveals his Light. Male energy wants to share its Light in order to fulfill the Vessel.

A kabbalistic concept known as The Three-Column System describes the underlying forces at play in the universe: The Force of Sharing (the right column), The Force of Receiving (the left column), and the balancing of these two energies, which is the Desire to Receive for the Sake of Sharing (the central column). It is through the energy of the central column—through our ability to Receive for the Sake of Sharing—that we create circuitry in a relationship. These three parts satisfy the functions of a negative pole, a positive pole, and a filament needed in order to give light.

Love in Motion

There are a lot of commonly held beliefs out there about love and relationships that are just plain wrong. I don't mean this as a judgment. I mean it as a simple observation about what works and what doesn't. One of the most misunderstood areas that could use the most rethinking is sex.

No other area of a couple's life offers more potential for embarrassment, hurt, and rejection than sex. No wonder couples find it such a challenge to communicate clearly about their sexual needs. Often when couples have this discussion, their conversations are indirect, imprecise, and ultimately, inconclusive. A lot of people feel insecure when it comes to whether their spouse finds them attractive or worry if they are a good lover, which means it's not easy to talk about sex. Many couples fall into the trap of discussing difficult topics at night in the bedroom, then withhold sex from one another as a form of punishment. Don't bring your disagreements into the bedroom. You don't want negative feelings associated with the room of love, comfort, and passion. Sex shouldn't be used as a weapon or anything other than an expression of sharing and openness.

Talking successfully about sex requires the conversation to be gentle and safe. Your partner will not know what excites you or what you may be uncomfortable with unless you express it. In order to talk about sex, couples must do the work I've mentioned previously to become vulnerable. To have a fulfilling sex life, both partners have to be willing to risk exposing their deepest insecurities to experience that intimacy that lies at the heart of the strongest relationship and the best sex.

Some people feel that having to ask for affection or discuss their sexual wants takes all the romance out of sex. I encourage you to instead, look at the longing behind the desire. For instance, if a man wants his partner to be more spontaneous in the bedroom, she may interpret that as his wanting someone wild, when he's just saying that he wants to try something new with the person he loves. If she expresses a sexual need, he may take it to mean that he hasn't been satisfying her and see it as an insult to his performance and virility, although she is just describing what would feel good to her. Often, one may misunderstand their partner's desire as a lack on their part. What they don't recognize is that what lies behind the words is the longing for greater intimacy.

When it stops being about "me" and starts being about "we," each person desires to please the other. Then they can hear their partner's yearnings in this deeper way. Giving their partner pleasure gives them pleasure. When the ego is set aside, you feel gratitude for this feedback instead of insecurity or rejection. It doesn't mean that you have to fulfill all their sexual desires, needs, and fantasies, but you want to be open to share and hear anything. The critical factor is always to hear the longing behind the desire.

Rethink Moment

- How do you indicate to your partner that you want to try something new?

- How does your partner let you know this?

- What messages do you think you send your partner when you don't acknowledge his or her wants?

- How do you think this might make your partner feel?

- How do you feel when your partner doesn't acknowledge what you want?

- How do you think you might introduce some lightness, levity, and fun—and therefore more creativity—into your lovemaking?

We often hear that the most important sex organ is the brain and that the biggest is the skin, which is why touch is so important.

Typically, women want and desire emotional closeness to feel sexual. For men, it's often the other way around. They need sexual intimacy to feel emotionally close.

As an example of this, one couple experienced a miscarriage after a six-month pregnancy. This was devastating for both of them, but they grieved in very different ways. The wife was depressed, and when her husband wanted sex soon after her miscarriage, she became angry. His intention was not to conceive another child, but rather to connect to her emotionally. For him, physical intimacy was a means of achieving emotional intimacy and the way he knew best to offer her comfort and reassurance. In contrast, she had no desire to have sex with him. Although she loved him deeply, she froze every time he touched her or made sexual advances. A woman can become averse to a man touching her if she thinks he's touching her just because he wants sex. She needed to feel emotionally connected to him in order to experience sexual desire. Once she was given the space to express her feelings of loss and grief to him, she began to desire him again.

Making love is an expression that can and should elevate your relationship and connection to a higher realm. Making love is an act of sharing, while having sex is connected to the ego, and includes the need for power, control, and selfishness. When sex becomes an act of instant gratification, there is no lovemaking in it. It becomes routine and, eventually, the magic is gone, leaving us at a loss as to why.

KABBALISTIC PRINCIPLE:

Sex is a sacred act. Through the love
we make, we contribute to the elevation
of our souls and the entire world.

. . . .

You Believe What?

Let's dispel a few damaging beliefs about sex.

MYTH: Most married people don't have sex regularly.
If you are telling yourself that the lack of passion in the bedroom is natural between married couples, then not only are you lying to yourself, but your statistics aren't entirely accurate! A 2010 Kinsey Institute survey revealed that 25% of married couples between 25 and 59 years of age have sex 2 to 3 times a week.[78] That's 1 in 4 couples, and that's a good place to start for one fundamental reason: Everything that happens in the bedroom is a reflection of the relationship. If your relationship is healthy, your sex life is healthy. If partners are generous outside the bedroom, you can bet they are generous

in the bedroom. Unfortunately, it's the same conversely—withholding and stingy partners exhibit the same behaviors between the sheets.

The British Journal of Psychology reported on a study that correlates altruistic actions with having more sex.[79] John Gottman found that when men share responsibility in household chores and childrearing, they and their partner have more sex.[80] This isn't only because the partner now has more time or is less tired; it's a reflection of how their partnership works. Life has a lot of responsibilities, and part of a successful relationship is feeling like you're not alone in bearing them. You want a partner who is there not only when it's easy, but also when it's exhausting. Couples who share responsibilities share the fun, too. Couples, where both partners have an equal share in *all* their responsibilities, reported the highest relationship satisfaction.

MYTH: My single friends are having more sex, and the sex is better.
Study after study shows that couples in long-term relationships have more sex than single people. Only 5% of singles reported having sex 2 to 3 times a week, compared to 25% of married couples. Furthermore, couples surveyed consistently report that they derive more pleasure from sex than their single counterparts. This assessment holds for both men and women. This is likely because couples who have a strong foundation of trust will naturally feel more connected to their mates, leading to greater feelings of sexual fulfillment.

MYTH: Couples can be in a happy marriage and not have sex.
I guess it all depends on how you define happy. If one or both partners are ill or cannot physically exert themselves, I am not suggesting that they shouldn't stay together. However, if two healthy people are in a relationship, live together, and yet do not have sex, they sound more like roommates than lovers. Somewhere, there is a problem. "It's just sex, and there is so much more to a marriage than sex," some might argue. I go back to my initial thought—a couple's sex life is a reflection of the relationship. People do not have sex solely for pleasure, nor strictly for procreation. Overwhelmingly, people seek out sex for connectedness. Humans are fundamentally and exceptionally social. If an orgasm were the only goal, there are more efficient and practical means of obtaining one. Sex is a social exchange. At its best, it is an expression of physical and emotional intimacy. Every time a couple

has sex, they strengthen their social bond with each other, creating greater unity and deepening their love. Fulfillment arises from shared cooperation and vulnerability, from expressing a deep and meaningful bond. The good news is that the more you have sex, the more you want it. Sex releases feel-good hormones, which in turn boost your libido, making you want more.

MYTH: Sexual performance is important.
Almost every aspect of sexual activity can be assigned a matching baseball metaphor. First base, second base, third base, home run; if someone rejects an advance, they have "struck out"; if someone's advance is not rejected, they "score." Where do I start with the problems with this metaphor? Most troubling is that it presents sex as a goal-oriented activity and ultimately a competition.

Sadly, many do see sex as a "performance" on which they will be judged with a win or a loss. Neither gender is immune to these superficial notions of sex. We all feel immense pressure to be sexy and to excel at sex, but sex isn't sport. It's not a means to an end. Assigning ideas of performance and competitiveness to the bedroom is a sure way to nurture self-consciousness and decrease sexual satisfaction, as well as damage intimacy.

Static in the Bedroom

Sexual imagery and content is everywhere. Much is written in the media about the potential hazards of all this sex on the impressionable minds of children. It does have an effect, but just as alarming is the impact it has on adults. We all derive our understanding of acceptable sexual mores and practices from what we see and hear. We also are very aware of what is considered sexy. Comparing ourselves and finding certain aspects lacking is detrimental, inevitably leading to inhibitions and embarrassment, neither of which are conducive to intimacy. How can you truly express love to your partner if your mind is fixated on what you hate about yourself?

Many partners bring baggage from past sexual relationships into the present. This is not surprising when the average age in the U.S. to have sex for the first time is 17. [81] More shocking (to me at least) is that 25% of teens have sex at age 15. [82] Rationally, most would agree that a 15-year-old is nowhere near mature enough to emotionally or cognitively make healthy decisions regarding sexual partners. Which is why years later when we look back on our youthful choices we wonder, "What was I thinking!?" usually followed by feelings of regret.

Sadly, there are very real repercussions for having sexual relationships at too young an age. Studies report that people who lose their virginity earlier in life have lower expectations for their sexual partners. Those who have sex after they turn 20 are more likely to have happy relationships. Often people who have sex in their teens end up settling in later relationships. This isn't always true, but for many, sex is confused with the emotional intimacy they are craving. Often this leads to an unhealthy relationship with sex. People who wait to have sex tend to have greater self-worth and higher expectations for their life partner.

Bottom line, people have different feelings about their past choices. Some see their past as a learning experience that brought them to the present, whereas others are ashamed of their past. Check yourself and see how you feel about your choices. If you are feeling shame, then work on changing that emotion because you can't change your past. Shame may be affecting you in ways you haven't been aware of, such as lowering your expectations for what kind of partner you deserve, to keeping you from having a genuinely pleasurable sex life.

Kabbalistic Practices

While there is no magical age when sexual intercourse becomes suddenly healthy, as opposed to potentially damaging, Kabbalah does stress the importance of choosing the right partner. Sex isn't just sharing intimately on a physical level—it has a spiritual dimension, as well. Even kissing creates a spiritual connection between two souls. Every person, every soul in this world, has a specific purpose and unique challenges that they are meant to face. Therefore, when we engage in sex, we take on a part of our partner's spiritual work (tikkune) and they ours. This is a very beautiful concept when we're in loving, long-term, committed relationships, but is distinctly less enchanting when seen through the lens of someone with many casual sexual partners.

This is a lot to take in, I realize. But if you're married, you're all set, nothing to worry about, right? Hardly! Kabbalists have long taught that specific energies are available at certain times. According to the kabbalistic lunisolar calendar, days, weeks, and even months are identified as possessing positive, negative, or neutral energy. The lunar calendar informs us when best to start new projects, get married, have surgery, and even, you guessed it, procreate.

There are myriad guidelines for spiritual lovemaking, and many focus on the timing of the act itself. Per the kabbalistic calendar, negative days are to be avoided, as are days when Aunt Flo is visiting. Or as the Danish say, "When there are communists in the funhouse." Or as the French say, "When the British are coming." Put literally, during menstruation. This period of abstaining goes on to include the seven days after a menstrual cycle, which roughly works out to 12 days a month of no intercourse. Like many who hear this for the first time, you may be thinking this is less a guide for having sex than one for NOT having sex! Let me assure you, the kabbalists were no fools.

As mentioned earlier, men, energetically, represent the Right Column energy of sharing, and women represent the Left Column energy of receiving. They connect to the Central Column by using restriction, the power to resist the immediate flow of energy that goes from one to the other. It is that restriction which reveals Light. Understanding the Three-Column System and the circuitry that can be created with male and female energy offers us the opportunity to create lasting joy and satisfaction in a relationship.

How many long-married couples do you know who are dissatisfied with their sex lives? Most, probably, if not all. At best, sex is predictable. At worst, one or both partners are engaging in emotional or physical affairs outside the marriage. The beauty of abstaining for nearly two weeks of the month is that when partners come back together, it is as if for the first time. There is anticipation, planning, and preparation every single month. You don't take sex, or each other, for granted. Think of it as an amazing return on investment from a little restraint.

Chapter Twenty Three

Happy Relationships Are Based on Deep Friendship

"It is not a lack of love, but a lack of friendship that makes unhappy marriages." — Friedrich Nietzsche [83]

. . . .

Happy relationships rely far more on how much fun you have as a couple rather than successful conflict resolution.

Universal throughout humanity is a desire for the profound bond of friendship, which can teach us about life and ourselves if we're open to it. A good friend is a staunch supporter and honest advisor, who challenges us to pursue our dreams and be our absolute best. Friendship is the connection between people when they feel seen, heard, and valued. Friends give and receive without judgment and derive strength from the relationship. The definition of friendship is much the same as the definition of a happy marriage. Friendship fuels the flame of love because it offers the best protection against feeling adversarial toward your spouse despite inevitable disagreements. Friends set aside their desire to vent and choose instead to defuse the situation because they prioritize the relationship over a momentary outburst.

When positive thoughts outweigh the negative feelings, it takes much more significant conflict to lose your equilibrium as a couple. Couples who put this into practice are generally more hopeful. They look forward to spending their lives together, and when obstacles arise, they give each other the benefit of the doubt.

Very often in relationships, we focus on:
- What the other person can give us
- How sensitive they are to our needs
- How consistent they are with their expressions of love.

To be a great friend, we must first look at ourselves to see what it is that we are creating for the other person. This is one of the many counter-intuitive teachings of Kabbalah: If you want something, you have to first give it.

Rethink Moment

• What amount of time do you spend smiling during your conversations?

• Do you show interest in what your partner shares with you?

• Is your demeanor open and engaged?

KABBALISTIC PRINCIPLE:

Friends are beloved as they do not turn away from the other and are one of life's true and lasting pleasures.

. . . .

Be Available

Many couples are unaware of the crucial role that small, mundane, everyday moments play in the stability of the relationship. The most obvious things often go unnoticed. Much the way I do, Michael enjoys sharing things with me that he thinks I would enjoy or find humorous. I might be busy working in the other room, with the kids, or have my hands full of cookie dough when he calls from the other room, "Come see this, I think you'll really enjoy it." "Right now? I have my hands full of cookie dough."

He'll say, "Yeah, I think you'll find this really funny."

I can say that 100% of the time, I stop what I'm doing, hands covered in cookie dough, to share that moment with him. It may not be the most convenient time, but he stopped what he was doing, thought of me, and wanted to share something with me, so I want to reciprocate. Those instances when you drop everything to connect even in the smallest way are the glue that binds you together in a hectic life. Close relationships consist of a series of emotional advances, which is when your partner reaches out for emotional connection, which can be displayed with a kind word, a smile, solicitation of advice, and sincere interest in what the other is doing or saying.

Whatever love we might feel in our hearts, others will only see in our actions.

Now, this may seem inconsequential, but on the contrary, when we engage in these exchanges, we are creating connection, all of which deepens friendship. To sustain your connection, everyday interactions shouldn't be taken for granted. This awareness will make an enormous difference in your relationship. Whereas, continually rebuffing or ignoring your partner's advances harms the relationship. Kind of obvious, I know.

For couples that live unhappily together, these moments are rare: more often the wife doesn't pay attention to what her husband is offering, or if she does, the husband doesn't even acknowledge her response and vice versa. The next time your partner wants to share and asks for your attention, give it to them. Drop everything, even if just for a moment. Share little moments of your day with your partner. Next time you pick up the phone to call a friend to share something that just happened, call your partner first. Repeat daily.

Big Change: Your Opportunity for Deep Friendship

Love is the nourishment humans need to fulfill their greatness. By not defining what that greatness is, we don't limit the possibilities. Let's face it, things happen in life that reveal character and make or break a relationship. We've all heard people say, "I thought I knew my partner, but this situation showed his true character." Usually, this is brought on by a change of fate. For me, the way my son, Josh, entered the world is a good example. From pregnancy to Josh's birth, through his diagnosis and the months that followed, I experienced a rollercoaster of emotions. It was an incredibly trying time for me, as it was for Michael, and it was challenging for us as a couple. I grappled with my feelings of failure, of being damaged. I created distance between us because I didn't know how to share those feelings. I didn't yet feel safe with that level of vulnerability because, in many ways, I had never experienced anything like it.

But through it all, Michael was my best friend. Through the pain and the struggle, I gained new clarity. I started to see the distance I had maintained between us by believing that the only person I could trust was myself; trusting anyone else wasn't safe. This was a dynamic that I saw as a child, so when I created my own family, I emulated it. I had always tried to be strong, taking pride in my ability not to need anybody else; I wanted to prove that whatever it was, I could do it on my own. But I came to realize that this was just ego at work, a defense mechanism I had created during childhood. Now I could clearly see that it had no place in my marriage.

After Josh's diagnosis, I let that all go, and Michael was there for me in ways that I could never have imagined. As my heart broke open, his love mended it back together and filled it with the sweetness of his own heart. From that point on, our relationship grew to a new level and set the course for the future. It wasn't until Josh was born that we learned how much we truly loved one another, with a depth and understanding, unlike anything I had ever known.

How have Michael and I emerged from this stronger and more deeply in love than we were before? It's simple. We decided that nothing was greater than our love for each other. Nothing. Not an argument, not being right. No matter what, our commitment to each other came first. Looking back at our marriage before Josh, I can barely recognize the couple we were then. We did what couples do, and over twenty-two years, we created a life together.

As we evolved, so did our relationship.

In the months after Josh was born Michael and I felt that we needed to laugh more. We weren't unhappy, but we were certainly serious, busy making plans for the future, figuring out how to best support Josh, and understandably, we lost some of our levity. One of the things I have always loved most about our relationship is that we often laugh and have fun together. We committed to trying some new things—in our case, it was tennis and salsa lessons, (Michael spent more time dancing with the male instructor than he did with me, as he needed a little more one-on-one teaching), we went for hikes, and rode bikes on the boardwalk. We laughed a lot in this process, but after two months of doing something every night, we were exhausted! The point is we made the time to have fun. We still make an effort to do new things together, which creates connection and intimacy and brings more joy to the relationship.

Instead of focusing on the challenges in your relationship, reframe your thoughts, and practice having fun.

"Against the assault of laughter nothing can stand." — Mark Twain [84]

Friends have fun together. Often couples are so mired in their routines and being proper, responsible "grown-ups" that they forget how to have fun or to try new things. They begin to resent day-to-day responsibilities and try to recreate the fun times they had when they were single. The courtship shouldn't stop once you get married or have kids. Travel the world together and explore new things, share exciting ideas, and keep discovering life, because that journey never ends.

Often we take ourselves and the negative things we do or say very seriously, and then we take very seriously the steps we have to take to repair that negativity. A great way to tackle the difficult task of diminishing ego is to make fun of ourselves.

When you look back at your day or week, do you see things you need to change, or are you at the level where you can see how silly your actions were? Realize it's not actually you—because there's a big disparity between who you are and who you are meant to be. You will find that you wish you hadn't done certain things—like yell at your spouse, lash out at someone at work, or get offended—you can choose to make a change instead of beating yourself up about it.

Taking change too seriously engages the ego, whereas treating it with levity and identifying your silly behavior doesn't invite the ego's participation. When you come to a point where you can laugh at yourself and the poor choices you made, through that levity you can create lasting change.

When my daughter Miriam was a year old and my sons Josh and David were two and six, our family was invited to a birthday party for the child of a couple we had recently befriended. We were looking forward to attending, and the relationship was new enough that we wanted to be sure to respond to the social overture by showing up. We got the children into the car and headed for the party with plenty of time to spare, but this was one of those times when the best-laid plans go astray. Our new friend's home turned out to be in a part of Los Angeles I had never been to before, complete with a warren of small streets and poorly marked intersections.

All this took place before smart phones were invented, and GPS was still an expensive rarity, so we certainly didn't have one in our car. Before long, we were not just lost, but hopelessly bewildered. As we drove around and around the unfamiliar streets, the children became hungry, one had a wet diaper, one had a spoiled diaper, and they were all bored and peevish. I know there are lots of jokes about husbands not asking for directions in situations like this, but even if my husband had wanted to, there was no one around to ask. In the meantime, to put it diplomatically, dark energy was beginning to make itself felt in the car. I was thinking my husband should have gotten better directions, to which I know he would have answered that getting directions was not necessarily his exclusive responsibility. Happily, none of those accusations were actually said!

This was not a life-or-death predicament, but small things can become big very quickly. Eventually, I pulled the car over to the side of the road and cut off the engine. Our immediate reaction was to vent frustration, but when our eyes met each other, there was a shift. We recognized that we both came to the same thought that this was just about a birthday party. Our smiling eyes instantly diffused the tension. We surrendered to the moment instead of trying to control it. Being totally lost, confronted with a hot car, cranky babies, and poopy diapers, we just lost it, but instead of losing it in a negative way, we thought it was the funniest thing and started laughing uncontrollably.

"Anyone can be passionate, but it takes real lovers to be silly."
— Rose Franken [85]

It was the second time in our marriage we'd been able to initiate such a profound shift. The first took place during the weeks following Josh's birth, when Michael and I made a pact that no situation is bigger than our relationship and commitment to each other. From the moment Josh was born, we had a choice to either let his diagnosis divide us or to use it as a way to become closer and more unified. We chose the latter, which marked a huge step forward in our relationship. In the car that day, when we were on our last straw, we looked at each other and compared to the real heaviness and overwhelmingly dark period we had just experienced, we couldn't take this challenge seriously. In light of everything that had happened, this felt like a paper cut. We gave up on trying to find the party but rather than writing off the day, or writing off each other, we started our day over.

The uncomfortable truth is that some couples will never resolve certain issues, but that doesn't mean that their relationship doesn't work or that they shouldn't be together. An issue has the power to be divisive only if they let it. There's always a choice to have a good laugh and draw closer together instead.

I know a couple whose relationship is working. They are British, and perhaps this is humor that only some people will get, but they shared this inside joke which illustrates what is at the core of their success as a couple. They say that if one of them came home one day and said, "I just killed somebody," the other would respond, "Ok, where do we bury the body?" This is not to say they are actual killers, obviously, but shows how unified they are. Rather than judge or blame their partner's grave error, they know that they have each other's backs no matter what.

My husband and I gave a lecture together, and at one point while Michael was discussing the importance of friendship and laughter, he said, "Just being up here with Monica makes me happy." I think that's the whole point.

"Of all the things that wisdom provides for living one's entire life in happiness, the greatest by far is the possession of friendship." — Epicurus

217

Chapter Twenty Four

Practice Makes Perfect

In an interview, a famous classical cellist, who had been playing at the highest level for fifty years, remarked, "It's strange, in ten or fifteen minutes I could tell you everything I know about playing this instrument, but it would be of little use to you. It has taken me a lifetime to discover these things. No matter what I tell you, I have no doubt that it would take you a lifetime, as well." I don't claim to have mastered the art of love the way this musician has mastered the cello, but I do believe that some of the most important principles in life and love can be stated simply—much more so than putting them into practice.

I'm going to let you in on a little secret. When I got married, I thought I was the perfect wife. I'm a Virgo, and we usually aim for perfection, so seeing myself as less than accomplished in this area just wasn't an option. Because I'd done such an excellent job of finding the right person to spend my life with, naturally, I was also right about what it meant to be a good wife. Much later in my marriage, I would come to realize how naive I was.

Although falling in love is an experience we all cherish, romantic love doesn't do the heavy lifting. Staying in love requires many expressions of generous behavior, and as relationships evolve and usually progress into marriage and perhaps children, cooperation becomes essential. This alone will not be enough to hold together a relationship over decades. A deeper kind of love grounded in compassion, forgiveness, loyalty, tolerance, and respect must emerge.

It's not enough to find "the one" if you're not going to invest in each other once you're together. A good analogy is that of a couple who had problems conceiving and spent years struggling with infertility, but then once the baby finally arrived, they never cared for or nurtured the child. That would be ludicrous.

Despite what you may think, when you get married, you're not a perfect husband or wife. It will take years of practice to even become good at it. Newlyweds, in their first year of marriage, are derailed when arguments occur. They say things like, "I didn't do anything wrong, I don't deserve this! I'm a good husband or wife." But the truth is you're not! Why assume that you're great at something you've never mastered? This is new territory. We all have the potential to be amazing, but it still requires continuous work and awareness.

If you're a thoughtful parent, you worry that you might mess up with the first child, so you check yourself now and again. How damaging are my choices to this child I'm responsible for? If we approached marriage with this consciousness, we'd be much further ahead than most couples.

KABBALISTIC PRINCIPLE:

Nothing worthwhile is attained by chance,
it must be pursued with unwavering effort and
perseverance. It is not enough to know something.
It requires continual practice to change through it
and become a different person.

· · · · · · · ·

A lot of scientific research has shown that if we want to excel at something, it's the trying and failing that enables us to reach our desired outcome. We think we know the roles a wife and husband should play from our parents, our culture, and T.V.

We grew up watching shows that created a vivid picture in our minds of just how easy marriage is. Remember June Cleaver, Mrs. Brady, and Mrs. Walton! Later, it was Peg Bundy and Edith Bunker giving us a completely different view of marriage! Both models set you up for failure, one with standards too high, and the other with standards too low. We have to throw away our misconceptions of what relationships are in order to embrace what they can be. We aren't taught how to create fulfilling relationships. Almost all other goals have a path that we follow. There are rules of the game, so to speak, specifically in regards to our careers, sports or banking, even learning to drive a car. Just as in these other things, love, too, is a rite of passage, but there is no manual.

Life is full of opportunities for learning how to love more. How do we do that? The same way that great cellist did. We practice. In that way, marriage is like anything else that you want to be good at. Learning to be a good partner (or for that matter, sharing a bathroom!) takes a certain dogged patience. It's tempting to look at other people's successful marriages and think they caught a break, but it's not just luck; it's practice. According to Malcolm Gladwell in his book *Outliers: The Story of Success* getting good at something takes 10,000 hours, and in case you're wondering, that's ten years! [86]

Half of all divorces occur in the first seven years of marriage (and research shows that most of these couples only seek outside help in the sixth year). So let's stop for a moment and think about this: If it takes ten years to master anything, how much time are these couples devoting to making their marriage a success rather than a failure? Gladwell says, "Practice isn't the thing you do once you're good. It's the thing you do that makes you good." [87] The same can be said of relationships.

What makes a person a good artist, a good musician, or even a good person? Practice. Nothing else. The same principle applies to marriage. You won't start out as a perfect husband or wife, but you can spend the rest of your life becoming one—with practice.

Conclusion:

The ~~End~~ Beginning

When you choose to make a life with someone, it's like remodeling a house. You keep the things that you like, but you incorporate both of your unique styles, combining them like an architect's blueprint. This blueprint is what your relationship should look like. You each come with things that you love, that you enjoy, that you cherish, and you find a way to cohabitate. We've all heard the saying, "He (or she) wears the pants in the family." But I like to say, "We both wear shorts," because no one person should wear the pants; equal partners create marital unity. Decide what kind of relationship you want. Discuss, explore, and then live it because whatever we focus on grows. If you focus on what your partner is doing wrong or all the things that are lacking in your relationship, then you will get more of that. If you focus on what you need to work on to create lasting change, that process will lead to long-term fulfillment.

Like growth, commitment is an inside job; it's not a simple vow. It's a willingness stemming from an understanding that you and your partner's well-being are linked over the long-term.

Two people I love dearly and who impacted my life greatly passed while I was in the process of writing this book and the father I knew my whole life began to disappear due to the symptoms of Alzheimer's. This brought into sharp focus how short life is, and that there is too often a lack of appreciation for what we have. For too many, there is also a lack of urgency. If I have one message for my readers, it is this: Make your relationship work, or leave the relationship, because the bottom line is that life is too short to be unhappy, to live in mediocrity, or in that place of "it's ok, but it's not great."

In life, we will experience hard times and challenges, and it's wonderful to have the support of a partner to help you through it, but that isn't the ultimate point. Your goal is to live your best life, and a husband or wife is an important part of that experience.

Love is more than just a feeling. It's a process requiring continual attention.

Question — and try — everything.

Rethink your love.

About the Author

Mother, wife, sister, daughter, teacher, friend, author, cardio enthusiast & change junkie. Monica Berg integrates all that she is into her mission of empowering others to discover their unique gifts. Authentic and fearless, she reminds us of our extraordinary potential and pushes us onward with compassion and understanding.

While informed by her many years of kabbalistic study, Monica channels the powerful internal spark of Light living within us all. Monica also draws heavily on her own life experiences. She battled and overcame a debilitating eating disorder, and as a mother of four children, one of whom has special needs, she has become an outspoken advocate for him and others struggling to find their voice.

With humor, insight, and honesty, Monica shows people how to create a life in which they are living and loving as the powerful and fulfilled person they've always wanted to be. She inspires people to get excited about a lifestyle of change by showing them how to bring strength into even their most challenging situations by changing the one thing they can—themselves.

Monica Berg is the author of *Fear Is Not an Option,* blogs weekly at www.rethinklife.today, and serves as Chief Communications Officer for Kabbalah Centre International. She lives in New York with her husband Michael and their children David, Joshua, Miriam, and Abigail.

Acknowledgments

Thank you, Rav and Karen, for showing my first real-life love story. Your love transcends time and space. Witnessing your relationship made me know that pure, unconditional, lasting love could exist.

To Michael, whom I have already dedicated this book to...you make me ridiculously happy.

Thank you to my children David, Joshua, Miriam, and Abigail for teaching me how to give love and receive love. Nothing more. Nothing less. Absolutely everything. May you always live your lives leading with your heart, with unconditional love, kindness, care, compassion, and empathy. You will find one day that this is the purpose of a life well lived and well loved.

Liz, in writing this book, I discovered aspects of myself I hadn't known, but I also became reunited with an old friend, you. A friend I have known longer than I can comprehend. You make my life more fun, rich, and purposeful. As I've told you often, "I like you so much, like crazy a lot. I want a miniature you to keep in my pocket. I'd feed you muffin crumbs, and we could talk all day."

Dearest Annie, I love you and miss you. You are no longer in this world, but to me, you are of this world...always.

Peter Guzzardi, my editor, you imparted two valuable words that I live by. Unpack this! You have helped me embrace patience, process, and made me a better writer. Thank you.

To my tribe, Mom, Dad, Rebecca, and Jessica, thank you for loving me all of my life and making sure I always felt it.

Thank you, Kelly Milano, Sarah Hall PR and team, Jazmine Green, and everyone who has supported me through this labor of love.

And to all of you, my readers, you are the reason I've worked on this book for seven years. May the words on each page resonate with you and empower you to create your most profound love stories.

Endnotes

1 Baldwin, James. "'Fifth Avenue, Uptown' by James Baldwin." Esquire, Esquire, 11 Oct. 2017, www.esquire.com/news-politics/a3638/fifth-avenue-uptown/.

2 Elimelekh, Kl̀£alonimus Kl̀£almish ben. *A Student's Obligation: Advice from the Rebbe of the Warsaw Ghetto*. J. Aronson, 1991.

3 Elimelekh, Kl̀£alonimus Kl̀£almish ben. *A Student's Obligation: Advice from the Rebbe of the Warsaw Ghetto*. J. Aronson, 1991.

4 Fielding, Helen. *Bridget Jones's Diary*. Picador, 1996.

5 Elimelekh, Kl̀£alonimus Kl̀£almish ben, and Yehoshua Starret. *To Heal the Soul: The Spiritual Journal of a Chasidic Rebbe*. Rowman & Littlefield, 2004.

6 Allison, Jay, et al. *This I Believe: The Personal Philosophies of Remarkable Men and Women*. Picador/Henry Holt and Co., 2017.

7 Allison, Jay, et al. *This I Believe: The Personal Philosophies of Remarkable Men and Women*. Picador/Henry Holt and Co., 2017.

8 Berg, Michael. *Becoming Like God: Our Ultimate Destiny*. Kabbalah Learning Center, 2010.

9 "A Quote by Oscar Wilde." Goodreads, Goodreads, www.goodreads.com/quotes/19884-be-yourself-everyone-else-is-already-taken.

10 Weintraub, Pam. "How to Grow Up." Psychology Today, Sussex Publishers, 1 May 2012, www.psychologytoday.com/us/articles/201205/how-grow.

11 Brown, Brené. Daring Greatly: *How the Courage to Be Vulnerable Transforms the Way We Live, Love, Parent, and Lead*. Penguin Life, 2015.

12 Jobs, Steve. "Text of Steve Jobs' Commencement Address (2005)." Stanford University, Stanford News, 12 June 2017, news.stanford.edu/2005/06/14/jobs-061505/.

13 Jaquish, Barbara. "Longer Is Better? We Seem to Think So." University of Arkansas News, 2 Sept. 2010, news.uark.edu/articles/14579/longer-is-better-we-seem-to-think-so.

14 Gibbs, Nancy. "The State of the American Woman." Time, Time Inc., 14 Oct. 2009, content.time.com/time/specials/packages/article/0,28804,1930277_1930145_1930309,00.html.

15 Popova, Maria. "Buckminster Fuller's Brilliant Metaphor for the Greatest Key to Transformation and Growth." Brain Pickings, Brain Pickings, 13 July 2016, www.brainpickings.org/2015/08/21/buckminster-fuller-trim-tab/.

16 "A Quote by Mahatma Gandhi." Goodreads, Goodreads, www.goodreads.com/quotes/142891-as-human-beings-our-greatness-lies-not-so-much-in.

17 Whitney, Craig R. "Jeanne Calment, World's Elder, Dies at 122." The New York Times, The New York Times, 5 Aug. 1997, www.nytimes.com/1997/08/05/world/jeanne-calment-world-s-elder-dies-at-122.html.

18 Kato, Kaori, et al. "Positive Attitude towards Life and Emotional Expression as Personality Phenotypes for centenarians 2." Advances in Pediatrics., U.S. National Library of Medicine, 21 May 2012, www.ncbi.nlm.nih.gov/pmc/articles/PMC3384436/.

19 Berg, Philip S. *Wheels of a Soul*. Kabbalah Learning Centre, 1987.

20 "MADtv." MADtv, season 6, episode 24, Comedy Central, 12 May 2001.Rimer, Sara. "Happiness & Health." Obesity Prevention Source, 19 Feb. 2014, www.hsph.harvard.edu/news/magazine/happiness-stress-heart-disease/.

21 Tolle, Eckhart. *The Power of Now: a Guide to Spiritual Enlightenment*. Namaste, 1997.

22"Albert Einstein Quotes." BrainyQuote.com. Xplore Inc, 2018. 7 June 2018. https://www.brainyquote.com/quotes/albert_einstein_130982

23 Hay, Louise L. *You Can Heal Your Life*. Hay House, Inc., 2017.

24 Slovic, P., Finucane, M., Peters, E., & MacGregor, D. G. (2002). The affect heuristic. In T. Gilovich, D. Griffin, & D. Kahneman (Eds.), Heuristics and biases: The psychology of intuitive judgment (pp. 397-420). New York: Cambridge University Press

25 Zajonc, R. B. (1980). Feeling and thinking: Preferences need no inferences. American Psychologist, 35(2), 151-175.Newton, Phil. "Traumatic Brain Injury Leads to Problems with Emotional Processing."Psychology Today, Sussex Publishers, 3 Jan. 2010, www.psychologytoday.com/us/blog/mouse-man/201001/traumatic-brain-injury-leads-problems-emotional-processing.

26 Haidt, Jonathan. *The Happiness Hypothesis: Finding Modern Truth in Ancient Wisdom*. Basic Books, a Memberof the Perseus Books Group, 2006.

27 Haidt, Jonathan. *The Happiness Hypothesis: Finding Modern Truth in Ancient Wisdom*. Basic Books, a Member of the Perseus Books Group, 2006.

28 Brown, Brené. *Daring Greatly: How the Courage to Be Vulnerable Transforms the Way We Live, Love, Parent, and Lead*. Penguin Life, 2015.

29 Berglas, S, and E E Jones. "Drug Choice as a Self-Handicapping Strategy in Response to Noncontingent Success." Advances in Pediatrics., U.S. National Library of Medicine, Apr. 1978, www.ncbi.nlm.nih.gov/pubmed/650387.

30 Berglas, S, and E E Jones. "Drug Choice as a Self-Handicapping Strategy in Response to Noncontingent Success." Advances in Pediatrics., U.S. National Library of Medicine, Apr. 1978, www.ncbi.nlm.nih.gov/pubmed/650387.

31 Howard, Ron, director. Rush. Universal Studios, 2013.

32 Deford, Deborah, editor. Reader's Digest Quotable Quotes: Wit and Wisdom for All Occasions from America's Most Popular Magazine. Reader's Digest, 1997.

33 "Marriage and Divorce." Monitor on Psychology, American Psychological Association, www.apa.org/topics/divorce/.

34 Soul, Jimmy. If You Wanna Be Happy: the Very Best of Jimmy Soul.

35 Mann, Denise. "Pregnancy Brain: Myth or Reality?" WebMD, WebMD, www.webmd.com/baby/features/memory_lapse_it_may_be_pregnancy_brain#1.

36 Miller, Donald. *A Million Miles in a Thousand Years: What I Learned While Editing My Life*. Thomas Nelson, 2010.

37 Harry, Njideka U. "Nelson Mandela Taught Us the True Meaning of Social Entrepreneurship." The Huffington Post, TheHuffingtonPost.com, 15 Feb. 2014,

38 Chuck Palahniuk

39 "Excerpts From Rushdie's Address: 1,000 Days 'Trapped Inside a Metaphor'." The New York Times, The New York Times, 12 Dec. 1991, www.nytimes.com/1991/12/12/nyregion/excerpts-from-rushdie-s-address-1000-days-trapped-inside-a-metaphor.html.

40 Flanagan, Owen J. *Consciousness Reconsidered*. MIT Press, 1998.

41 Kiyosaki, Robert, and Sharon Lechter. *Rich Dad, Poor Dad*. Warner Books, 1997.

42 Marshall, Garry, director. Beaches. Touchstone Pictures, 1988

43 "The Freudian Theory of Personality." Journal Psyche, 2018, journalpsyche.org/the-freudian-theory-of-personality/.

44 History.com Staff. "Battles of Trenton and Princeton." History.com, A&E Television Networks, 2009, www.history.com/topics/american-revolution/battles-of-trenton-and-princeton.

45 "Vince Lombardi Quotes." BrainyQuote.com. Xplore Inc, 2018. 6 June 2018. https://www.brainyquote.com/quotes/vince_lombardi_100525

46 Billy Joel. Just the Way You Are, Columbia Records, Sept. 1977.

47 Gilbert, Daniel Todd. *Stumbling on Happiness*. Vintage Books, 2007.

48 Lisitsa, Ellie. "The Magic Relationship Ratio, According to Science." The Gottman Institute, The Gottman Institute, 15 Feb. 2018, www.gottman.com/blog/the-magic-relationship-ratio-according-science/.

49 Walsh, Coleen. "Money Spent on Others Can Buy Happiness." Harvard Gazette, Harvard Gazette, 17 Apr. 2008, news.harvard.edu/gazette/story/2008/04/money-spent-on-others-can-buy-happiness/.

50 D. W. Winnicott, *The Child, the Family, and the Outside World* Middlesex 1973

51 Berg, Rav. "The Unity of True Love." Zohar.com, The Kabbalah Centre, www.zohar.com/article/unity-true-love.

52 Berg, Michael. *Becoming Like God: Our Ultimate Destiny*. Kabbalah Learning Center, 2010.

53 Drigotas, S. M. (2002). The Michelangelo Phenomenon and Personal Well-being. Journal of Personality, 70, 55-77

54 Calhoun, Ada. "To Stay Married, Embrace Change." *The New York Times, The New York Times,* 21 Apr. 2017, www.nytimes.com/2017/04/21/style/modern-love-to-stay-married-embrace-change.html.

55 Bernstein, Rebecca. "Business Psychology: Golem Effect vs. Pygmalion Effect." BUonline, Management News, 14 Dec. 2017, online.brescia.edu/management-news/golem-effect-vs-pygmalion-effect/.

56 "You Bet Your Life." Dwan, Robert and Bernie Smith, directors. You Bet Your Life, performance by Groucho Marx, CBS Radio, 1955.

57 "Everybody Worships: David Foster Wallace on Real Freedom and the Skeleton of Every Great Story." Mockingbird, 18 June 2012, www.mbird.com/2008/09/more-david-foster-wallace-quotes/.

58 Callahan, Maureen. "The Night Tiger Woods Was Exposed as a Serial Cheater." New York Post, New York Post, 26 July 2017, nypost.com/2013/11/24/the-night-tiger-woods-was-exposed-as-a-serial-cheater/.

59 "Andre Maurois Quotes." BrainyQuote.com. Xplore Inc, 2018. 11 June 2018. https.//www.brainyquote.com/quotes/andre_maurois_107694

60 Fraley, r. Chris. "Adult Attachment Theory and Research." R. Chris Fraley, University of Illinois, 2018, labs.psychology.illinois.edu/~rcfraley/attachment.htm.

61 McCaffrey, Anne. *The Dragonriders of Pern*. Ballantine Books, 1968.

62 Schulz, Kathryn. "Being Wrong." *The New York Times, The New York Times,*10 June 2010, www.nytimes.com/2010/06/11/books/excerpt-being-wrong.html.

63 Gandhi, and S. Radhakrishnan. All Men Are Brothers: Life and Thoughts of Mahatma Gandhi. Literary Licensing, 2011.

64 Smedes, Lewis B. *Forgive and Forget: Healing the Hurts We Don't Deserve.* HarperOne, 2007.

65 Kabbalah Centre. "On Blessings and Gratitude." The Kabbalah Centre, The Kabbalah Centre, 1 Sept. 2015, kabbalah.com/en/concepts/on-blessings-and-gratitude.

66 Weingarten, Gene. "Pearls Before Breakfast: Can One of the Nation's Great Musicians Cut through the Fog of a D.C. Rush Hour? Let's Find Out." *The Washington Post,* WP Company, 8 Apr. 2007, www.washingtonpost.com/lifestyle/magazine/pearls-before-breakfast-can-one-of-the-nations-great-musicians-cut-through-the-fog-of-a-dc-rush-hour-lets-find-out/.

[67] Stillman, Jessica. "Gratitude Physically Changes Your Brain, New Study Says." Inc. com, Inc., 15 Jan. 2016, www.inc.com/jessica-stillman/the-amazing-way-gratitude-rewires-your-brain-for-happiness.html.

[68] "A Quote by Henry Winkler." Goodreads, Goodreads, www.goodreads.com/quotes/41593-assumptions-are-the-termites-of-relationships.

[69] Fulwiler, Michael. "The Empirical Basis for Gottman Method Couples Therapy." The Gottman Institute, The Gottman Institute , 13 Mar. 2017, www.gottman.com/blog/the-empirical-basis-for-gottman-method-couples-therapy/.

[70] McLeod, Saul. "Maslow's Hierarchy of Needs." Simply Psychology, Simply Psychology, 21 May 2018, www.simplypsychology.org/maslow.html.

[71] Burford, Michelle. "Women's Power to Hurt the Male Ego." CNN, Cable News Network, 25 Oct. 2010, www.cnn.com/2010/LIVING/10/25/o.glass.ego/index.html.

[72] "Red Skelton Quotes." BrainyQuote.com. Xplore Inc, 2018. 6 June 2018. https://www.brainyquote.com/quotes/red_skelton_391663

[73] Gottman, John Mordechai and Nan Silver. *The Seven Principles for Making Marriage Work*. Cassell Illustrated, 2018.

[74] Gottman, John Mordechai and Nan Silver. *The Seven Principles for Making Marriage Work*. Cassell Illustrated, 2018

[75] Cruz, Germano Vera, and Liria Maússe. "The Kinsey Institute (2010). National Survey of Sexual Health and Behavior. Indiana KI. - References - Scientific Research Publishing." Open Journal of Acoustics, Scientific Research Publishing, 19 Aug. 2014, www.scirp.org/(S(lz5mqp453edsnp55rrgjct55))/reference/ReferencesPapers.aspx?ReferenceID=1262827.

[76] Arnocky, Steven, et al. "Altruism Predicts Mating Success in Humans." Freshwater Biology, Wiley/Blackwell (10.1111), 18 July 2016, onlinelibrary.wiley.com/doi/abs/10.1111/bjop.12208.

[77] Sangwin, Becca. "4 Typical Solvable Relationship Problems." The Gottman Institute, The Gottman Institute , 2 Apr. 2018, www.gottman.com/blog/4-typical-solvable-problems-relationships/.

[78] Finer LB and Philbin JM, Trends in ages at key reproductive transitions in the United States, 1951–2010, Women's Health Issues, 2014, 24(3):e271–e279, doi:10.1016/j.whi.2014.02.002.

[79] Martinez GM and Abma JC, Sexual activity, contraceptive use, and childbearing of teenagers aged 15–19 in the United States, NCHS Data Brief, 2015, No. 209,

[80] "Friedrich Nietzsche Quotes." BrainyQuote.com. Xplore Inc, 2018. 10 June 2018. https://www.brainyquote.com/quotes/friedrich_nietzsche_109784

[81] Twain, Mark. *The Mysterious Stranger and Other Curious Tales*. Gramercy Books, 1997

82 "A Quote by Rose Franken." Goodreads, Goodreads,
www.goodreads.com/quotes/64672-anyone-can-be-passionate-but-it-takes-real-lovers-to.

83 Gladwell, Malcolm. *Outliers*. Penguin, 2009.

84 Gladwell, Malcolm. *Outliers*. Penguin, 2009.

Rethink Your love

Rethink Your Love

Rethink Your Love